The Compression Planning Advantage:
A Blueprint for Resolving Complex Issues
Institute Reference Manual

First Edition

Patrick McNellis

Does the slow pace of decision making in your organization frustrate you?

Does your organization have projects and issues that never seem to get resolved, projects that seldom get completed on time, or strategies that languish?

Available at:
CompressionPlanning.com &
Amazon.com
1-800-569-6018

'What People Say About Compression Planning'

"I was 28 years old (it was 1983) and asked to put together a group of experts from electric utilities to develop a national R&D plan. We hired Jerry to train our facilitators and I have been using his techniques ever since to run small, medium, and large meetings.

I believe Jerry's teaching and concepts have not just helped me in planning meetings but also in critical and strategic thinking. People are always amazed at how much we can get done in large groups with effective planning and facilitation."

Jonathan W. Hurwitch
Executive Vice President
Sentech, Inc.
Bethesda, MD

"Efficiency is what we were seeking; consensus is what we got as a byproduct. This is a very focused way of getting people on board.

The Board really liked it. Comments like 'this is exactly what we needed' were the rule vs. the exception.

Take any task – eliminate the what we are not here to address – outline what we need to do – get at the 'to do's' and get everyone to literally sign on for their role.

We have a construction project and a capital campaign - this process is very useful for both. We used the process for our Board retreat – the Board really liked it.

Focus – keep everyone on task.

You won't find a better group of people with whom to work and their experience makes the process extremely efficient and cost effective. It will save you a lot of meetings."

Raymond B. White
Chief Executive Officer
The Watson Institute
Sewickley, PA

"I first learned about Compression Planning in the early 1980s and have been using it since. We recently trained 18 colleagues to use Compression Planning and they are using it in a variety of ways. We've had sessions that clarified the organization of details for our new international campus, planned a move into a new building complete with thousands of details on a very short timeline, and prioritized daily activities."

Tom Botzman, Ph.D.
VP Business & Finance
St. Mary's College of Maryland
St. Mary's City, MD

"Every time I've used Compression Planning, it's been a huge time-saver for the participants. I'd say absolutely 75% savings in time."

Jay Duffy
Retired Dir., Executive Development and Leadership
Bayer Corporation
Pittsburgh, PA

"My purpose for learning the Compression Planning process was simple: an agency (National Institute of Corrections) who contracts with me uses the Compression Planning process on a fairly routine basis.

I was thrilled as I'd been impressed by how quickly NIC staff...utilizing the Compression Planning process...were able to develop very complete plans to solve fairly complex problems in very short periods of time.

The Compression Planning training is masterfully designed. Participants bring real-world projects and apply the Compression Planning process to those ideas, projects etc. The ability to take a goal (in some cases a thought) to a sold plan in a matter of a few hours and have truly great minds (the other participants) from a broad variety of back grounds help with the planning – what a deal!

This system has been one of the most valuable tools in my tool chest."

Winnie Ore
President, Western Training and Consulting
'Center of the Enhancement of Human Potential' LLC
Helena, MT

'What People Say About Compression Planning'

"Compression Planning really levels the playing field, and one of the things people like best about the process is it's fun! Many, many times I hear 'This is the best planning session I've ever been in.' It spans the gap for everyone. If you're no-nonsense, you'll like it for that reason. If you're creative, you'll like it because it allows you to be very creative and open to a lot of different directions."

Peter R. Hughes
Market Vice President - Business Development
Advocate Christ Medical Center
Advocate Hope Children's Hospital
Advocate Trinity Hospital
Oak Lawn, IL

"Most recently, we had the opportunity to use Compression planning in one of the LLC's that has a total of four partners. One of the partners is the managing partner and is at the business every day. The other three of us are there one day a month for guidance and consultation.

We needed the best way to herd cats. Each of the four partners are entrepreneurs and we needed to act collaboratively. We needed to get together to put a strategic plan together for 2008, and we only had one day to do it. Some parts of the plan are to increase sales by 20% (measurable) and improve throughput by 30% (measurable), and do it at the same cost.

The plan was put together in one day, with a planned one-day follow-up with two additional people to lay out some specific detail on equipment moves."

Bob McDemus
Partner, Reneuxit LLC
Westchester, PA

"I had seen first-hand many Compression Planning techniques used by a new supervisor who arrived at the College soon after my arrival. I was so impressed that when the College offered the opportunity to participate in the McNellis Compression Planning Institute I altered my vacation plans to attend.

I was certainly not disappointed and learned more than I had ever hoped toward getting to the root of an issue and arriving at a solution in a more effective and efficient manner."

George W. Waggoner
Director, Campus Technology Support Services
St. Mary's College of Maryland
St. Mary's City, MD

"I took the class back in the fall of 1988. I still have the binder and still refer to it. It was probably the most useful seminar in my career...stuff I could apply immediately.

The Compression Planning techniques I learned are key elements in starting our major projects. I see two big benefits of the techniques. One is the ability to compress the time it takes to get started. Without Compression Planning, we could probably collect all that stuff in other ways but it would take longer – in some cases, a lot longer. In other cases, it might be impossible.

The second benefit is that Compression Planning helps us reach consensus as a group. It's essential to get our clients in agreement and in some kind of alignment. The technique does that because all the decisions the group makes are visible and they're irrefutable. When we have agreement, we can move a project forward."

Don Moyer
Co-Founder, ThoughtForm Inc. - Information Architects
Pittsburgh PA
Among their many prestigious clients are Hamburger University at McDonald's, Steelcase, Caterpillar, BearingPoint, and Otis.

'What People Say About Compression Planning'

"I used Compression Planning through-out our Lean Six Sigma implementation at Dormont Manufacturing Company.

A key to success for any Six Sigma team is creativity and getting the input of all the resources on the team. Speed also helps the process to not falter and keeps team meetings productive. These are all hallmarks of Compression Planning. It was always my contention that every Black Belt (leaders of Lean Six Sigma Projects) should be a trained and experienced Compression Planning facilitator."

Michael A. Couch
President
Michael Couch & Associates Inc.
Pittsburgh, PA

"I've experienced the effectiveness of Compression Planning many times. It enables people to work in a much more efficient and effective manner and allows them to pursue more opportunities.

I know the investment in the training will be returned tenfold."

Pat Gerity Ph.D.
VP Cont. Ed/ Workforce & Community Dev.
Westmoreland County Community College
Youngwood, PA

"CP is at the base of everything I do. It's kind of like Lamaze. I got into it for one reason and then found applications for it in so many other aspects of my life. Sometimes faculty members have an idea of what they want to do and they're not really sure how to make it specific. How do they make it into a form that we can apply for a grant and fund their idea?

For example, one group I did Compression Planning with involved four cooperating organizations who wanted to help girls get more interested in science. We received a four-year grant for $800,000."

Pamela Jira
Executive Dir. Foundation/Assistant to the President
Zane State College
Zanesville, OH

"We've found CP really helpful in providing direction and priorities for the grants we apply for a yearly planning period. It helps get all the entities and departments on board for what we are going to do...the priorities...they buy in to the collective agenda and where we'll spend our efforts.

The biggest benefit for us has been to get people on the same page priority-wise. When you work in higher education, people have their own agendas with their own priorities. Compression Planning helps people see and appreciate the big picture in the mission of the larger university."

Chris Shaw
Grants and Projects Coordinator
Ohio University
Zanesville, OH

"I used CP to help teams of employees coming together from three different nuclear plants to develop common processes that would be implemented as the standard across our fleet. We worked on establishing common processes for everything from the procedures we use to perform work to how we make design modifications to nuclear power plants.

Besides being an effective tool, CP really did make a very difficult job a little easier for the folks involved. These employees were asked to develop these common processes in addition to their normal work so they were only able to come together periodically.

For these teams, CP was a life saver."

Jeanny Amidon
...in her work with First Energy
Toledo, OH

'What People Say About Compression Planning'

"We were approached by a school district to write a grant. It was really complex because it involved three federal agencies and a host of community partners. Doing a grant with one department of the federal government is tough enough. Working with three federal departments is unbelievably complex – and we only had two weeks to pull it all together and submit it.

The competition for the grant was fierce and people all over the country were applying for it. Their people had done lots of the background work that needed to be pulled together and focused. Everyone thought there wasn't a chance to get the grant; however, we took it on.

In two meetings...one for about two hours...another for one hour...we used Compression Planning and identified all the parts and pieces and most importantly, identified the holes...the gaps that were missing and assigned them to people to be completed.

I know without Compression Planning that school district and their partners would not have been awarded the $9 million grant."

John Jeanetta
Vice President of Organizational Development
AIM Institute
Omaha, NE

"Recently, the Boston Consulting Group released a study showing that 80% of CEOs think that innovation is critical to their future, but less than half of them think they are doing a good job with it. It also showed that we have lots and lots of good ideas, but were not commercializing them. To me that means there are probably one of two things happening. Either the good ideas aren't good enough to capture the imagination and passion of the people OR, they don't have a process in place to successfully implement ideas.

Compression Planning does both of those things. It can take a good idea and make it great...and it creates an environment that allows passion and engagement to emerge, which greatly enhances the likelihood of successful implementation."

Joyce Wycoff
Founder, InnovationNetwork
Bakersfield, CA

"Compression Planning is the core methodology in my consulting practice. It is what I am getting to be known for as a business consultant. I use it in one way or another in each and every one of my work engagements.

Use it with your family, with your church, at your work, in your personal decisions. Use it and you will find it to be a great tool to add to your life skills."

Alfredo Enrique Umaña
Director, Applied Consulting
Tegucigalpa, Honduras
Central America

"When you need quick decisions, when you're bringing a lot of diverse people to the table with different agendas and different motivations, Compression Planning keeps everyone focused on the target goals."

Mary Jo D'Orazio
Manager, Training and Organization Development
Services, Human Resources
Denver International Airport,
Denver, CO

"The Compression Planning System is by far the single-most effective tool I have learned in all of my travels through two masters degrees and a gazillion workshops."

Jan Nedin
Performance Solutions Architect
Five Star Development, Inc.
Pittsburgh, PA

"Frankly, I went to my first CP workshop as something of a skeptic. Many times, such workshops have provided interesting information and a chance to meet good people, but rarely do they live up to their billing.

In any case, I attended because I recognized that my work depended on the ability to get productive and timely work from groups. At the time, our state department of education had just mandated the development of comprehensive district plans in just about every area related to teaching and learning; each had a requirement for a quick turnaround and each one

'What People Say About Compression Planning'

required that the product—the plan—be the result of collaboration among faculty, administrators and parents.

I was looking for insights into group process and group dynamics—a few useful hints, perhaps. What I got was a very different way of looking at things, one that focused on results yet still provided those involved with the respect, dignity and opportunities for meaningful input they deserved. After completing the training, I was able to go back to my school district, work with diverse groups to develop the required plans, and include in those plans really meaningful goals, activities and program assessments.

I've been a proponent since then—and I've used it in countless ways: strategic planning, program design, program assessment, personnel evaluation, presentations to the community, and team building."

Robert Feirsen, Ed.D.
Superintendent
Garden City Public Schools
Garden City, NY

"Our work teams find this remarkable system has documented bottom-line results:
- Time to completion drops an estimated 50%
- Errors and mistakes drop an estimated 40%

Most importantly, a sense of total ownership for the process grows among employees '10 fold.' What makes this system particularly unique in today's over tech world is that it does this without the use of a computer, without any costly hardware.

What used to take us weeks now takes hours with the 'thinking technology' that drives the Compression Planning system."

Doug Hall
Founder and CEO of the world famous Eureka! Ranch
Newtown, OH
…uses the system to plan every inventing project he conducts for his impressive client list:
Nike, Walt Disney, Ford Motor Company, American Express, Hewlett Packard

"Jerry not only helped me to create a relationship with a group of people I had no experience with, but also turned that session into a results-oriented meeting that will generate benefits for some time to come. He did an excellent job of staying on task to make sure we accomplished what I had intended from this session and then generated a document that helped us follow-up in the weeks and months ahead. Thanks Jerry!!"

Scott Schrank
Vice President, Hampton Brand Management
Hilton Hotels Corporation
Memphis, TN

"I worked for a large public relations agency that was asked to constantly write proposals, which took a lot of thinking and agency time to develop. Some clients would hire us, but a lot of people would simply steal our ideas and recommendations.

Compression Planning helped us solve this problem, not as a brainstorming means for ourselves but as a product we would offer clients. We sold it as the 'first step' in working with a client. We used it to explore their current situation, brainstorm possible solutions and prioritize a set of recommendations.

Compression Planning solved two problems. First, it allowed us to get paid for writing a proposal (about $5,000 for a two-hour session with two to three agency and two to three client representatives). Second, our proposal acceptance went way up, because we were now giving recommendations and we already had a chance to start proving ourselves in the kick-off meeting.

Since that time, I've used CP frequently for strategic planning, developing marketing plans and other consensus-building activities. It continues to work great and continues to turn unpaid meetings into events that clients love and that produce results."

Lloyd Corder, Ph.D.
President & CEO
CorCom, Inc.
Pittsburgh, PA

'What People Say About Compression Planning'

"The project was for the Air Force because they wanted to determine whether Saddam Hussein was detonating any nuclear devices.

Six of us did a Compression Planning session – a machine shop supervisor, two machinists, one sheet metal mechanic, Dr. Shell and I. As a young scientist, Dr. Shell was involved with the Manhattan Project that built the first atomic bomb.

We storyboarded for about two-thirds of a day and planned the whole thing! When we went out of there, we knew exactly what we wanted. We knew what specific pieces of instrumentation we needed. We knew how we had to have everything mounted. We had everything we needed to start construction.

The Air Force was able to take air samples and feed it through our device to tell whether any nuclear gases, as a result of nuclear fission, were released into the atmosphere. The air samples could be taken from 1,000 miles away from the site they wanted to check."
Don Bolland
Owner, Bolland Machine
Chippewa Township, PA

"I was looking for something that was new and unique to planning. I needed something that was different than writing on flip charts where we had no way to organize or develop an action plan.

Part of my job with the Bureau of Prisons as the Distance Learning Administrator is to produce all Satellite-Internet Broadcasts, where we produce all types of training and I use Compression Planning to plan the programs.

There are so many ways that this can be used. I am pushing to convince my administration to use this method with all the unnecessary meetings that we must sit through.

You could use this method to plan a multibillion dollar project to a small project."
Edward C Wolahan
Correctional Program Specialist
Dept. of Justice, National Institute of Corrections
Aurora, CO

"Jerry McNellis and Compression Planning allowed us to develop a team and transition our small company from a crisis-driven managed organization to a proactive, growing international company. Using Jerry's techniques, we opened up communications across all lines of the company and destroyed those 'silos' that get in the way of being great.

Compression Planning not only gets your team excited to change, but forces you to execute that change. We are a small food company with great products in a niche business. We were structured to react to customer needs. We lacked the controls and standard operating procedures to grow profitably.

Compression Planning helped us implement needed controls to strive to obtain our corporate vision, while living under our values and mission. With controls in place and the right team, we have had significant growth. Jerry McNellis and Compression Planning laid the groundwork to allow us to achieve our success."
Edward H. Schaefer
President/C.E.O.
Silver Spring Foods/Bookbinder Foods
Eau Claire, WI

"Compression Planning fell into my lap and I am glad it did. It has been, by far, the best professional development opportunity I have had in many years. The approach is fresh, sensible and credible – it works. I use this strategy in practically all aspects of my work...beyond formal Compression Planning sessions. In particular, I use it in planning trainings and meetings. I am using CP with a number of school districts in strategic planning or improvement planning.

I have used it with other groups as well to solve problems, kick-start stale plans and plan major events. The results of all my sessions have been surprisingly great. I am not sure why I continue to be surprised, but I do. People walk away from sessions thrilled with the product(s) generated – they love having a plan of action."
Dr. Judy Reault
Assistant Superintendent, Teaching and Learning
Educational Service District 123
Pasco, WA

'What People Say About Compression Planning'

"I estimate we complete projects in about a third less time with Compression Planning. The process allows us to be one of the most productive grants offices in the United States. There are only two staff members in our office, and last year we completed 188 projects. Over 22 years, we've received $118 million in successful grants. Compression Planning gives us a huge competitive edge. We use it on 100% of all major grants and projects.

We academics have a reputation for discussing things to death. We are exceptional at sitting around and admiring the problem. We want to look at all possible options, and end up solidly bogged down. Compression Planning enables us to avoid that and focus quickly on the key strategic things."

Neil Herbkersman
Senior Director of Grants Development
Sinclair Community College
Dayton, OH

"A one-day Compression Planning session to help a commercial aircraft flight software client 'focus its product value proposition' yielded – within three weeks of implementation – new contracts with the Sprint/Nextel corporate fleet, Honeywell, Worldspan, Goodrich, and Navaro giving an exponential leap for the small firm's revenues and long-term contracts.

The focused action plan from a one-day Compression Planning session helped a nonprofit foundation client achieve a 35% increase in annual donations within the first five months of its 12-month plan."

Brian Cubarney
Founder and Creative Director, ClearBrands, Inc.
Zelienople, PA

"Jerry McNellis has broken the code on focus and effectiveness in team planning. Compression Planning is the most effective collaboration tool that I have used – it builds teamwork, and simply gets things done. It is a gem of a tool for leaders who want to build collaborative teams, authentic consensus, and effective follow-through. Mastering this planning skill is well worth the effort.

If you want shorter meetings, authentic team consensus, and clear ownership and follow-through on tasks, Compression Planning is for you. Your team meetings will never be the same! (thank goodness!)"

Dan Chaverin
Executive Pastor
Westside Family Church
Lenexa, KS

"When a project needs collaboration, I know of no better way to define and establish that collaboration so that each partner takes ownership and feels good about her/his roll than using Compression Planning.

There is ALWAYS new, and sometimes surprising, information uncovered that strengthen one's application."

Blaise E. Favara, M.D.
South Valley Pediatrics & South Valley Child and Family Center
Hamilton, MT

"I have used Compression Planning for over 20 years at three companies. It is a great tool to bring people together to find an answer to anything from problems to vacation planning. When a team of people come together in this atmosphere and learn the method, they are unstoppable in finding and agreeing on a solution."

Les Whitver
Vice President, Michigan Seamless Tube
South Lyon, MI

"*Exploding the Meeting Myth* is the result of many years of experience, as Jerry McNellis has fine-tuned his breakthrough methodologies of how a leader can transform an organization and the process by which strategy is identified, planned and conducted (or implemented).

His concepts are focused, engaging of all, fun and highly effective in their capacity to produce results. I recommend his vision for organizational effectiveness – made practical in every sense of detail – to CEOs, division or department heads, planning executives, pastors, or anyone in a position to harness the help of others to

'What People Say About Compression Planning'

produce an end result. Jerry's methodologies are fresh and innovative, with the capacity to infuse an infectious form of energy into a team of people, whether it is a small group or large organization, wide-ranging or narrow in scope."

Bob Speck
President/CEO
Blue Coast Burrito
Brentwood, TN

"The CP Institute training was like turning a light on for me. I leaned the essential skills to become a more effective facilitator. I currently assist my company's internal strategic planning group by serving as a CP facilitator for a wide variety of cross-functional issues. I most recently used a CP session to help the Legal department to identify the formal processes and critical steps needed to manage contracts and legal documents. The goal was to prioritize the processes in order to more effectively introduce a document management information system.

The key concept I learned from CP is the importance of having a purpose, a non-purpose and background for each and every meeting. I have sat in too many meetings where time is wasted because every participant has a different idea of what is to be accomplished. CP teaches that getting everyone on the same page at the beginning of a meeting is essential if you are going to ask that group to address a topic or solve a problem."

Bryan A. Pai
Systems Analyst
SunEdison
Beltsville, MD

"I have experienced and used Compression Planning for over 25 years. How do you describe the indescribable – you don't – you need to experience it. If you get one message from this book, it must be 'I need to go and experience this!!'

From church retreat, to corporate board, to professional organization, to academic institution, to multiservice defense research project, to a family vacation – all are enhanced and enabled by this process.

The interactive and communication playing field is leveled as each participate – irrespective of rank or status – and has the opportunity for equal influence since the process ensures that ideas not individuals win the day and determine the future."

Trevor Macpherson M.D.
Professor of Pathology and Vice Chair Pathology
Medical Education
Residency and Fellowship Program Director
Department of Pathology
University of Pittsburgh Medical Center
Pittsburgh, PA

"In my role as Director of Planning and Grants at a large, public technical college, Compression Planning has been instrumental both in the development of an institution-wide strategic plan and in planning programs and grant projects. I have also successfully used Compression Planning with various smaller nonprofit organizations to develop program and fundraising action plans.

In every situation where I use this approach, people who participate are delighted with the outcomes they achieve in a short period of time, and they are always energized by the process and appreciate the relationships that emerge from this positive experience. And in the debriefing process, it's clear that people feel valued by having used their limited time wisely and productively. This is absolutely the best approach to planning I have seen in any organization!"

Sula J. Hurley
Director Office of Planning and Grants
Greenville SC Technical College
Greenville, SC

"Over the past 10 years, I have leveraged Compression Planning to drive powerful outcomes to critical decisions and thinking in both corporate and nonprofit environments. The logic behind the Compression Planning approach brings the best out in meeting participants in a transparent, democratic way. Some powerful insights have emerged from Compression Planning sessions.

The genius behind Compression Planning is much more than a unique way to facilitate meetings. Compression

'What People Say About Compression Planning'

Planning starts by understanding the basic human needs of recognition, certainty, variety, growth, contribution and connection. The secret sauce of Compression Planning is that it plays to basic human needs and builds on participant strengths.

I have found Compression Planning to be a welcome remedy to emotionally charged topics. It works again and again. Perhaps that's why I've had Jerry train numerous leaders and associates numerous times over the years."

**Chris Padgett
Corporate Director of Marketing
Humana Inc.
Louisville, KY**

"I was introduced to Compression Planning in 2005 and attended the Advanced Institute in 2008. If anything, I waited too long before attending the second meeting!

Compression Planning is truly a unique way of thinking and I have used it in developing mission, vision, values statements for both non-profit and for-profit organizations. Our clients have found the CP sessions to be both intuitive and energizing.

Intuitive in the sense that the structure and rules make complete sense, and energizing in the sense that they are cognitively liberating – enabling participants to take larger steps in thinking and decision-making in less time than they might otherwise."

**David Fortt
Founder, New Image Associates
Tolland, CT**

"We were hired by an area university to help with a problem they were stymied with. They tried to develop a specific program for two years, but they kept going around in circles. With one Compression Planning session, they were finally able to generate action steps that they had struggled to come up with for two years."

**Dr. Morris Beverage
President
Lakeland Community College
Kirtland, OH**

"I first encountered Jerry McNellis and his methodology for addressing issues while working for the General Motors EV1 program. The EV1 was an invention-on-demand program that required quick, thoughtful action to address problems, define alternatives and build electric vehicle solutions. Jerry's method for capturing ideas, focusing discussions and enhancing ideas to encompass more than simple thoughts provided the means for our team to define the future.

The Compression Planning process is simple to implement and results in team cohesiveness. It is so much easier to build the future with your team aligned to a common purpose. An action plan built with commitment to incorporate input from all players is a plan with a greater chance for success. This process provides that result.

I have personally utilized the process to determine my future career plans with great success. Jerry is a mentor I respect and admire who suggested that this approach could be used to capture the myriad of thoughts surrounding any subject including personal planning. I gave it a shot and it worked. I use it for everything from defining bylaws for a cabin community to next career positioning. Thank you, Jerry, for your enlightenment. I recommend that others take the opportunity to grow and try the process to clarify their world."

**Laurel Castiglione
Former Manager, Web Governance, Globalization and Marketplace; Corporate Communications
General Motors Corporation
Proprietor, Castiglione Enterprises, LLC**

"I was just trained in Compression Planning this last summer of 2008 during my year-and-a-half stay in the United States. Very enthusiastic about the concept and what I have learned, I was sure that it would not only work in the US but also in Europe.

The perfect occasion occurred when we had a retreat of our family-owned Forest Management Company 'Boscor Forest' that manages roundabout 30,000 acres of forest land in Germany and Austria. There were six forest engineers, three administrators, three members of the senior management team, plus me as the 'independent' facilitator. The goal was to identify critical issues in our

'What People Say About Compression Planning'

day-to-day business in the following areas: Forestry (Production), Administration and Management.

After a day-and-a-half of storyboarding and a lot of fun we came up with five key problems that we needed to address in the next year to improve our outcomes as well as detailed plans that outlined the action steps to solve each problem.

At first, the Germans were very skeptical. In the end, very enthusiastic about Compression Planning and what we had achieved: no more wood production without storyboarding!!"

Constantin von Reizenstein
Ph.D. Student in HealthCare Economics
University of Munich
Co-Owner of a German Forest Estate

"The logic of coordinated group problem solving is too often trumped by the associated burden. In *Exploding the Meeting Myth*, Jerry McNellis outlines a thoughtful process used successfully with countless organizations over three decades. The bottom-line is quicker and smarter answers that address fundamental organizational problems and opportunities.

But in the Compression Planning process so much more is gained. Learning with peers becomes a reality. The ability to see issues with clarity and to sift quickly through volumes of data and information is improved.

The process also highlights a key failure in organizational development—deciding what not to do. And importantly, the methods outlined can be used regularly throughout the year with efficiency and speed."

Steve Moya
Former CMO, Humana, Inc.
Santa Barbara, CA

"My husband Marc and I returned to the Philippines two weeks ago, and the first thing we did was to start a Compression Planning session. We had each gathered snippets of information from different sources on our two-month trip in the US, and wanted to share them as part of the background for our planning.

We then moved to our non-purposes, and sure enough there were about 10. We were left with the one thing we had to focus on as we returned. Within two hours we had defined our task, the parameters which needed to be met and within four days we had accomplished that goal and were ready to plan again.

It was the NONs that helped us focus and get complete agreement so quickly."

Suzanne Jacobson
Training Consultant
Manila, Philippines

"We'd been through a very difficult transition in our college, and felt the need to begin healing the institution. We decided that strategic planning was to be the vehicle for bringing people together, and we chose Compression Planning with Jerry McNellis as the model for our process. We trained 17 people as Compression Planning facilitators and this group evolved into the institution's Planning Council.

With Jerry's assistance, we conducted a series of external focus groups and ultimately, decided the best approach was to put every employee in the college through Compression Planning simultaneously. We did 14 sessions concurrently, for more than 300 people in one day. It was a way to demonstrate across the college that we were serious in our commitment to transform the institution and that we were serious about our employees being part of the process.

We were so pleased with the outcome that we now use Compression Planning in a variety of ways, other than just strategic planning for the institution. We're using it in work with our Advisory Committees, working with some of our internal committees and councils and in curriculum planning. We're starting to use it in work we do with some of the external organizations in our communities. We are adapting the process to our institution and are extremely pleased with the successes we are having.

We've given voice to a group of people who felt they did not previously have a voice in the organization. Compression Planning created a framework allowing us to address thorny issues in a positive, productive

'What People Say About Compression Planning'

manner. Very quickly, people realized they were being given power and they demonstrated their commitment by taking ownership of the process and outcomes. It kept them in an active role. We've had members of the staff stay they've never worked in an organization where they felt as valued as they do now. That's a powerful statement.

I've been in the administration of higher education for over 30 years. The day the Planning Council presented the Vision, Mission, Values and Goals developed through the Compression Planning process to the College's Board of Trustees was probably the single most emotional day in the life of an institution that I have seen in my career. I have never felt prouder of an organization in my life.

I knew intuitively there would be a strengthening of the institution resulting from our experience with Compression Planning. I don't think any of us expected the power, strength and commitment we've seen. We've gotten far more out of the experience than we anticipated. We're now in a good place and we're becoming a stronger institution through our work with Jerry and Compression Planning.

Trust the process of Compression Planning. At the end of the day, if you stay with the process, it will get you where you want to go."

Joe Forrester
President, Community College of Beaver County
Monaca, PA

"I used Compression Planning with our board to set priorities for the areas we would pursue for grants. Frequently working with such groups is like herding cats and CP helps rein them in and get people focused and committed.

CP helped make the ideas concrete/specific. It was an interdisciplinary group...academic and community members."

Joan Haley
SW Area Health Education Center & Coordinator
Pittsburgh Schweitzer Fellows Program
Pittsburgh, PA

"Compression Planning - A Million Dollar Idea

Dear Jerry,

Thank you so much for your Compression Planning seminar I attended last year at Robert Morris University. It has been helpful to me personally and professionally. As a result of that seminar, I've led several sessions in our company and your techniques have proven to be quite useful in helping us generate new marketing ideas.

You'll be interested to know that one idea that came out of one planning session helped develop an idea that generated over $1,000,000 with a single email promotion in less than a week.

I led a Compression Planning brainstorming meeting in Delray Beach, Florida with a few top level copywriters who work with me at Agora, Inc. Agora publishes financial analysis and advice for individual investors. The purpose of the meeting was to generate new headline and lead ideas for promotions. Out of that two-hour meeting came four ideas worth further development for our products.

One of the ideas that came from the brainstorming session was further developed by an editor/copywriter into a promotion for a $10,000 financial product to be sold via the Internet. That one promotion alone generated over 100 orders in less than a week. You do the math. That's over a million dollars.

This was an unusually successful promotion behind a very big idea for an expensive product. A typical email promotion may generate $35,000 to as much as $100,000. So this got a lot of attention. It didn't come without a lot of effort (and also a few headaches), but still the results were remarkable.

Since that planning session, there has been a much greater interest in using Compression Planning for other divisions of our company.

Thom Hickling (deceased)
Freelance writer for Agora Inc.

'What People Say About Compression Planning'

"Several things happened during my first CP session. First, even though I had always received compliments on my facilitation skills, I was taken aback by the participation of each group and how good they felt at the end of the sessions.

Second, we got twice as much accomplished than with my old process and no one left wondering about the next steps.

And, finally, we didn't have to figure out how one newsprint stuck on the wall related to another because the CP boards and cards were organized…they were right in front of us and easy to build on in preparing our next session and next proposal draft. I was sold!

I find the preplanning session with the key stakeholders invaluable. By having this session in place, the first session with multiple stakeholders is so much more productive and people participating really appreciate the clarity of the bigger picture.

We're using CP with every single proposal that we develop. I do know that we have improved the time it takes us to develop most grants by eliminating duplication of effort and not having to backtrack to find out something that we missed.

The 'old dogs' like me who have problems learning 'new tricks' need to know that this will bring a breath of fresh air to your work and you'll wonder where it has been all of your life. Just think about the fact that people will walk away feeling good about the meeting (how often does that happen?) and they will be talking about how skillful you are to others."

Judith Cawhorn
Executive Director of Grant Development
Mott Community College
Flint, MI

"It began innocently enough over two decades ago at a professional society retreat. The stated aim of said retreat was to update the society's strategic plan. Anticipating the usual fruitless and boring meeting with colleagues, I reluctantly agreed to participate. Two days later, the society had a new future roadmap, every participant was energized and engaged, and I was a changed person. The meeting was facilitated by Jerry McNellis and his colleagues from the Compression Planning Institute. It was my introduction to the power of the Compression Planning methodology.

Enthralled by the outcome of that meeting, I attended a training session determined to learn the basic principles. I returned to my home institution as an enthusiastic proponent. Within months I facilitated any number of disparate planning sessions – from re-designing the psychiatry department to exploring the hospital's role in fetal medicine. Each proved so successful that we invited Jerry to train a wider group of facilitators at the hospital. I have employed Compression Planning in such diverse settings as nonprofit organizations, schools, and professional groups, all the way to the personal level of selling our home.

Of all the tools and techniques I have learned over the years, the only one that has endured, matured and evolved to where it is as useful today as it was when I was first exposed to it, has been Compression Planning. It is adaptable to a wide variety of planning and problem solving issues. Regardless of the latest management fad du jour, Compression Planning can be employed with success."

Denis R Benjamin B.Sc., M.B.,B.Ch
Medical Director of Pathology and Laboratories
Cook Children's Medical Center
Fort Worth, TX

Past President – Society for Pediatric Pathology
(a.k.a. The Cowtown Curmudgeon)

'What People Say About Compression Planning'

"Compression Planning is the single most effective thinking strategy and group planning and problem solving technique I have ever learned. Learning the process profoundly changed the way I planned and thought through every part of my life. In the over twenty years I have been using the process I have led hundreds of group planning sessions around the country. Without exception attendees are amazed at how much gets accomplished in so little time and how fully engaged everyone is.

When I was hired as CEO I integrated the process into our way of doing business. Our staff are trained and we have trained and disseminated the technique to hundreds of people within our community and around the state. The return on investment in learning and using this process is so astronomical I can't even attempt to calculate it."

Luanne J. Panacek
Chief Executive Officer
Children's Board of Hillsborough County
Tampa, FL

"As a believer and user of Compression Planning, it has become a very valuable tool in our project management toolkit. We have adapted the CP structure and principles to the planning and execution of our IT projects. We have applied it in all phases of project management, including work breakdown sessions, daily team meetings, problem solving, and project retrospectives. The power of the tool for us is that:

- It provides a framework that is adaptable to a variety of applications.
- It creates a visual platform for information.
- It is persistent...we can work on it, stop, and come back to it. Team members can add things 'on-the-fly' for discussion with the group at a later time."

Jack R. Rearick, PMP
Project Management Office
Federated Services Company
Pittsburgh, PA

"Jerry and his team have done several strategic planning retreats for our clients, who are comprised of physicians and researchers primarily in academia. If any of our clients ever wants an outstanding, reasonably priced team to lead their strategic planning efforts, Jerry McNellis and Compression Planning are at the top of the list of our recommendations.

Jerry spends a fair amount of time interviewing participants in advance of the meeting, reading the association's literature, and is extremely prepared for the retreats. The design that goes into planning a retreat is so well thought out, and collaborative, that, in the end, we've always gotten a phenomenal product that has helped moved the organizations to the next level. The systems used are simply outstanding.

We recently had a retreat with Jerry and his team that involved some very complex issues. Jerry's firm, yet warm style, helped us work through these issues. And, it was actually quite fun in doing so! I consider Jerry a top-notch facilitator and a friend whom I highly respect."

Laura Degnon, CAE
Vice President, Degnon Associates
McLean, VA

"My very first reaction to reading the chapter on "'Pure Form Thinking'" and going through your course is that it is the cornerstone concept.

I thought that you detailed the various thought processes well and gave plenty of real-world suggestions and examples.

You always keep it real.

Reading the chapter brought me back to your session (almost live)."

William Safian
Director of Business Development
Advocate Health System/Trinity Hospital
Chicago, IL

'What People Say About Compression Planning'

"Sometime in the late 1970's, my boss sent me to a three-hour seminar with some guy named Jerry McNellis on Compression Planning. I was a typical frustrated Human Resources guy in an analytical, formal, engineering environment. The frustration came from the 'analysis paralysis' that such organizations fostered.

But Compression Planning became a real source of energy and personal motivation that has served my career and ambition very well for the last 30 years.

The analytical people in the organization came to love the process, its speed and its effectiveness. When I realized the impact this tool could have on organizations, it became my ticket to a truly unique career path as a professional facilitator with a product that really worked. And it worked every time.

Compression Planning has allowed me to build a business practice around strategic planning for boards of directors and trustees of major organizations and associations throughout the country. Since 1991, we've helped over 700 groups put together their strategies for future success.

When I think back, I didn't even want to go to that seminar."

Pete Clifford
President, Advanced Leadership Services
Columbus, OH

"On one level, *Exploding the Meeting Myth* by Jerry McNellis is a traditional 'how-to' business book, albeit an exceptionally well-written one. It compares favorably with the many business best sellers that I've read over the years. Each chapter has been researched well, there are many real-world examples of how to put his insights to use, and the reader is presented with lots of logical, thorough examples of how to take a simple business meeting and turn it into a series of actionable steps. Simply viewed as a 'how- to' manual, the book is a fine addition to any business library.

Like an onion, though, it has other layers beneath its surface. McNellis takes the reader on a journey. Early on in the book, it becomes very clear that he is the 'Yoda' of planning, facilitating, and mastering the business meeting. Among the many thoughtful tips and observations, the reader also finds a straightforward commentary on 21st century business culture underlying the main message of this book. The message truly is insightful and, makes the book relevant to a wide audience. He takes on topics such as the team workplace, pureform thinking, how to focus on the real issues, and how to dig for rich ideas.

What I find most appealing about *Exploding the Meeting Myth* is how McNellis manages to integrate his interpretations in a way that prevents these important themes from becoming overbearing or preachy. He doesn't smack you over the head with his views; he simply guides you through some very insightful observations. Well done!"

Tedd Long
Principal, National Practice Leader
HR Innovation
Findley Davies, Inc.
Toledo, OH

"*Exploding the Meeting Myth* is a comprehensive and thoroughly enjoyable introduction to Compression Planning. It describes the ingeniously simple process that not only facilitates problem-solving, but also builds consensus and buy-in for even the most challenging issues.

Compression Planning has been an important tool in our firm's tool box for more than 20 years. We've used it to help clients design school buildings, plan promotional campaigns, facilitate a community investment plan for a major non-profit, and develop countless management strategies.

Author Jerry McNellis made his reputation as a highly stimulating and engaging presenter and facilitator. McNellis' personal observations and highly instructive case studies translate easily to the pages of *Exploding the Meeting Myth*. In highly readable style, this book provides a practical, real-world process for addressing virtually any issue with speed and clarity."

Mark Luetke
President, FLS Marketing
Toledo, Ohio OH

'What People Say About Compression Planning'

"Before receiving training in Compression Planning, I attended many meetings where the facilitator used this process. I found those meetings much more productive and focused, and with a pre-defined outcome when we completed our task.

My favorite part of Compression Planning is the communication plan.

It specifies the minute steps that the group must take to ensure that their plan is implemented with fidelity. It gives the group confidence that its hard work and wonderful ideas will actually be communicated, which adds accountability to ensure that the tasks will be completed!"

Carrie Bearden, Ph.D
Director of Exceptional Children
Ohio Valley Educational Cooperative
Shelbyville, KY

"Compression Planning is a 'spirit and energy audit' for leaders who will make a difference in their organizations. Jerry McNellis is the Yoda master of Compression Planning.

It's no secret now how he does it. Although he has his own magic to add, Jerry offers the Compression Planning Process for leaders who know that there is more they can give and more that their teams can give. Over the past twenty-five years, I have used this process and I know there is no better set of guidelines and concepts to develop teams and, generate plans, than Compression Planning. Every month, I use this process and I see the 'sprit and energy' of a team reemerge.

I know it works. I have worked with thousands of leaders, from corporations to religious communities to individuals who were spiritless and depleted of energy. This process brings an invitation to 'invest in the best ideas for the right reasons right here - right now.'

Compression Planning infuses confidence, sets direction, and in these scary financial times, Compression Planning provides the GPS way through the tough issues for organizations and leaders."

Nancy T. Foltz, Ph.D.
Pittsburgh, PA

"Compression Planning has played a role quietly behind the scenes of several initiatives over almost 20 years within Luxottica Retail (we're better known for our LensCrafters, Pearle Vision, Sunglass Hut, Sears Optical and Target Optical retail brands). We enlisted Jerry and his team years ago to help craft the early LensCrafters brand corporate mission, vision and core values; we've since used the process on multiple initiatives, from identifying streamlining opportunities to executing innovative ideas that delivered eyeglasses to more needy recipients during international optical missions. We've found Compression Planning very effective in taking initiatives from idea to action in a way that builds collaboration and consensus.

Luxottica Retail places heavy importance on leadership at all levels. As part of our leadership philosophy, we believe in challenging the process and enabling our associates to act. In a tough retail business climate, like other organizations we're faced with doing more, with fewer resources, in the least possible time. Once again, we've enlisted McNellis for high-impact workshops to help us equip a targeted pool of associates with Compression Planning skills. In a recent workshop, about 20 participants worked on real projects with an estimated price tag of almost $50 million. These participants, many with multi-million dollar business responsibilities, have begun to report powerful productivity gains. Some are moving projects forward by two months or more by conducting a single two-hour compression planning session.

Jerry McNellis and team have truly developed a 'thinking technology' that has proven effective for our organization over time, and now, we're incorporating it more than ever to empower associates, drive personal productivity, provide handrails for delivering results and developing leaders."

Annette Brown, Professional Development Specialist
Mary Pater, Director Talent Management
Luxottica Retail
Mason, OH

Compression Planning Workbook Table of Contents

Setting the Stage
Seminar Purposes.................................. 1
Cornerstone Deliverables........................ 2
Compression Planning Definition.............. 3

Compression Planning
The "Storyboard" System........................... 4

Master Planning Model
Single Master Planning Model...................5
Single Model with Template Headers......... 6
Double Model with Template Headers....... 7
Timing Suggestions................................8-11

Pure Form Thinking
Background and Explanation................... 12
Phrases... 13

Design
Overview... 14
Design Template....................................15
Topic Card... 16
Purpose of this Session.......................... 17
Non-Purpose of this Session...................18-20
Overall Purpose....................................21
Background... 22
Permission Meter..................................23
Headers.. 24
Boundary Questions.............................. 25
Revisit Design......................................26
Design Evaluation Form......................... 27
Action Verbs.. 28
Design Form..29

Models
Demonstration Model #1.......................30-34
Demonstration Model #2.......................35-38
Demonstration Model #3.......................39-44
Demonstration Model #4 45-47

Headers
Examples.. 48-53
Formations... 54-61
Training Applications............................62-64

Facilitation
Process and Content..............................65
Facilitation Roles...................................66
Facilitation Tips....................................67
Neutral Facilitation............................... 68
Keep a Session Moving..........................69
Large Groups.......................................70-72
Spinning...73-74
Off-Site Facilitation............................... 75-80

Concept
Focusing into Concept............................81
Concept Headers..................................82-83
Supplemental Notes..............................84-85
Decision Assist Grid............................... 86

Action Plan
Instructions... 87
Action Planning Options........................ 88-91
Micro Planning.....................................92
FAQ..93

Communication Plan
Instructions...94
Wedding Example................................. 95-99

Debrief
Instructions...100

Uniqueness
Process.. 101
Fundraising Example.............................102-109

Project Teams
Definition of Roles................................110
Recruiting Project Teams.......................111
Models... 112-117

Getting Started
Do's and Don'ts....................................118
Session Walk-Through...........................119

YAMA
Definition and History...........................120
Supplemental Notes..............................121

© McNellis & Associates • Compression Planning Institute • 724-847-2120 • www.compressionplanning.com

The Tools
The Space 122
Suspension System 123

Design Alert
Definition and Instructions 124-125
Supplemental Reading 126

Briefing Board
The System 127

Additional Resources
Generating a CP Report 128-134
Table-ology 135-143

In this Compression Planning Institute, we will build our learning around 6 cornerstones

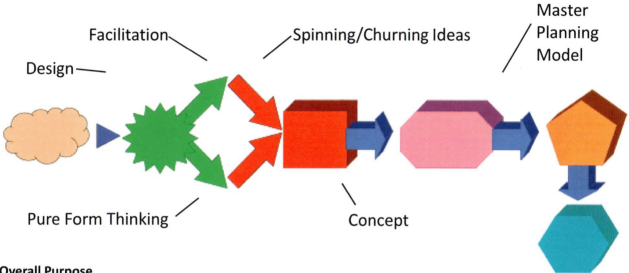

Overall Purpose
- To successfully design and facilitate a two hour session with **8** to **12** participants using the Master Planning Model.

Purpose of this Seminar
- To be able to identify all phases of the **Master Planning Model** and to lead a Project Team through a planning session using the Master Planning Model.

- To be able to complete all elements of a **Design** using the diagnostic questioning process.

- To be able to understand **Pure Form Thinking** and to be able to explain the importance of separating the Exploring Phase from the Focusing Phase.

- To be able to fulfill the various roles of a **Facilitator** in the Master Planning Model and to manage the different energy levels of groups while serving as a skilled facilitator.

- To be able to incorporate **Spinning/Churning** of Ideas into the facilitation of a session as a way to develop thinking and to maximize the team's contributions.

- To be able to enable a Project Team to focus its ideas into a manageable few (well done) and to develop **Concept** headers which prioritize the ideas appropriate for the design/client.

Non-Purpose of this Seminar
- To train you to train others

Setting the Stage - Cornerstone Deliverables

Cornerstones	Knowledge	Attitudes	Skills
Pure Form Thinking	To know the difference between Exploring and Focusing	To respect the need for separating thought processes in sessions	To explain PFT to a group and manage it through facilitation
Master Planning Model	To identify the seven steps of the planning process	To gain confidence and comfort with the task at hand	To facilitate transition through the Master Planning Model
Design	To understand the 7 key elements of a complete design To know how to adapt the diagnostic questions to a specific issue	To respect the importance of focusing a groups energy and thinking through design To appreciate that the pathway to design is through diagnostic questioning	To complete a design that contains all the components of the Master Planning Model To work the clients responses and needs into a design
Facilitation	To transition and guide a group through the Master Planning Model To identify and respond to the energy level of the group	To have an attitude of flexibility and fluidity To be comfortable with different levels of group energy	To recognize the need for and be able to adjust a design To appropriately manage the energy level of the group
Spinning/ Churning of Ideas	To know the difference between spinning and brainstorming/listing	To value and appreciate spinning as a way of bringing out and building ideas through the additional contributions of the group	To distinguish the difference among raw thoughts and prototypeable ideas To use the phrases for spinning
Concept	To know the technique for focusing a group on key deliverables	To value the importance of the manageable few, done exceedingly well	To develop formation headers appropriate to the design/client To fulfill the client's expectations by meeting the designs deliverables

© McNellis & Associates • Compression Planning Institute • 724-847-2120 • www.compressionplanning.com

The Compression Planning® System

Definition:

"The McNellis approach is a visual group process designed to bring out a group's best thinking and energy to resolve a complex issue in an environment of fair play and equal participation led by a skilled facilitator.

Compression Planning gets everybody heading in the same direction and *compresses* the planning time for major projects to enable your organization to achieve the results you need."

The Compression Planning System using Storyboards

Purpose
- To help people and organizations think more effectively
- To increase meaningful involvement
- To dramatically speed up collaborative work

Origin
- Leonardo da Vinci
- Walt Disney
- Mike Vance
- The McNellis Company

Physical Characteristics
- Use Creative Covers ®
- Use 4'x4' Regular & Portable Folding Storyboards
- Use Mini Storyboards 24"x30"
- Use Easels
- Use J-Track (carpet track) to suspend boards
- Use cardstock, pins, markers, etc.

Major Uses
- Planning
- Strategic
- Long Range
- Project
- Cross Functional Groups
- Personal Teams
- Idea Development
- Problem finding and resolution
- Organizing
- Communicating

Physical Characteristics
- Planning centers/team rooms
- Business
- Home
- Conference Rooms
- Work Stations
- Hallways
- Retreat Sites
- Production Centers
- Almost Anywhere!!!

© McNellis & Associates • Compression Planning Institute • 724-847-2120 • www.compressionplanning.com

Single Master Planning Model

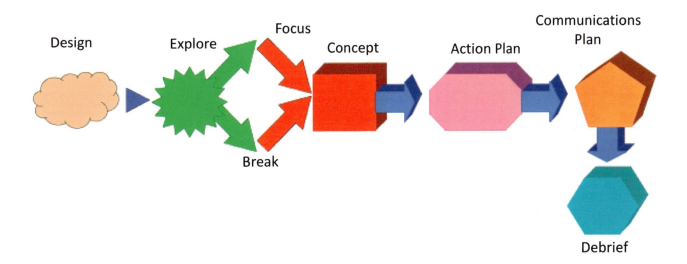

Single Master Planning Model

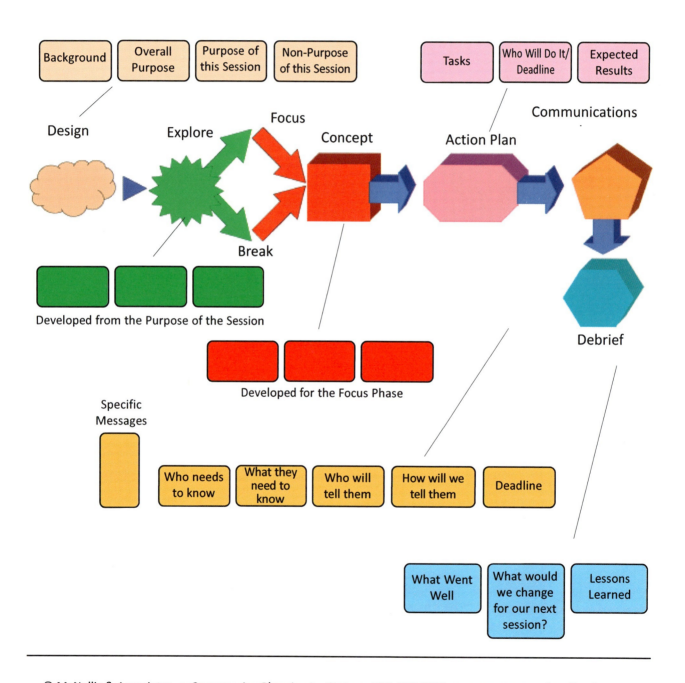

Double Master Planning Model

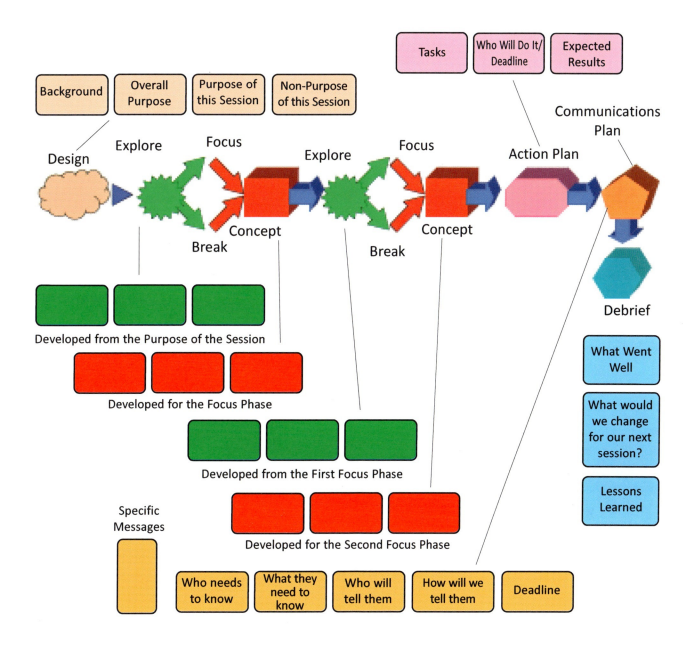

Suggested Timing
Single Master Planning Model - 2 hours

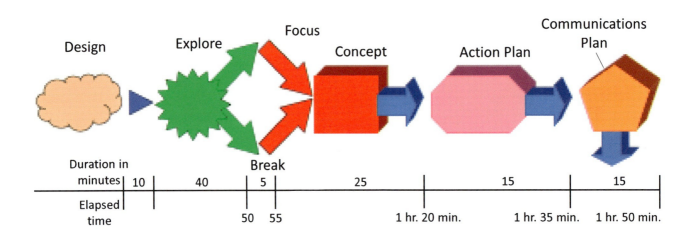

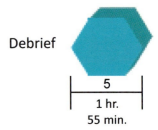

Suggested Timing
Single Master Planning Model - 4 hours

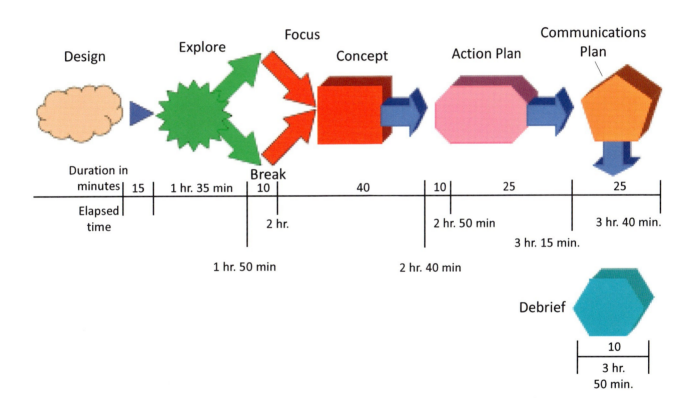

Suggested Timing
Double Master Planning Model - 2 hours

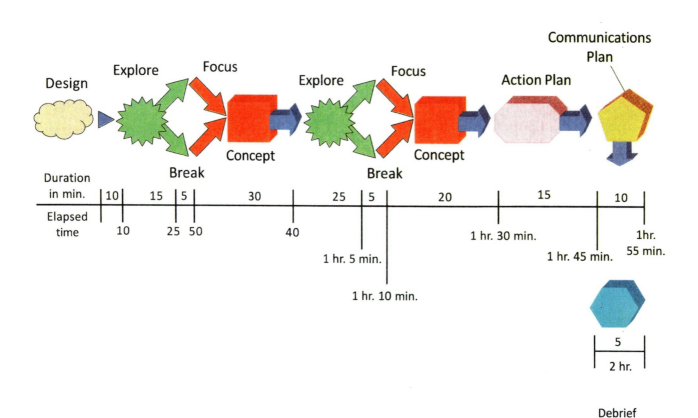

Debrief

Suggested Timing
Double Master Planning Model - 4 hours

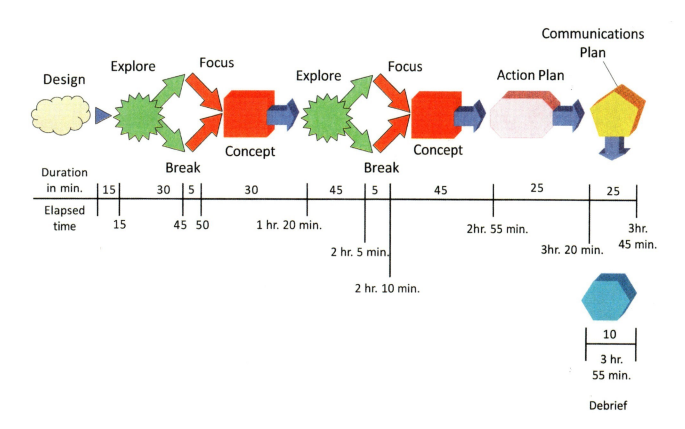

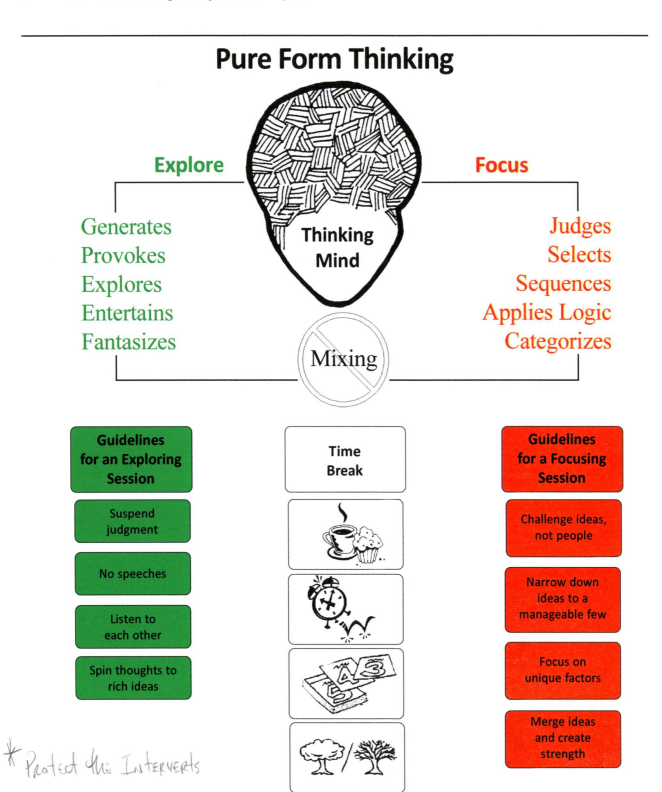

Pure Form Thinking - *Phrases*

Purpose: To turn off creativity when inappropriately applied

1. It's not in the budget	2. We're not ready for it	3. Everybody does it that way	4. Too hard to administer	5. Too theoretical
6. Production won't accept it	7. Personnel isn't ready for this	8. Not timely	9. The old people won't use it	10. The new people won't understand it
11. Takes too much time (work)	Don't move too fast	Has anyone else ever tried it?	Let's make a market test first	Let's form a committee
16. Won't work in our territory	17. Too big (or too small) for us	18. We don't have the right people	19. We tried that before	20. Too academic
It's a gimmick	You'll never sell that to management	Stretches the imagination too much	Let's wait and see	25. Too much trouble to get started
26. It's never been done before	27. The union will scream	28. Let's put it in writing	29. They...	30.

Non-verbals

© McNellis & Associates • Compression Planning Institute • 724-847-2120 • www.compressionplanning.com

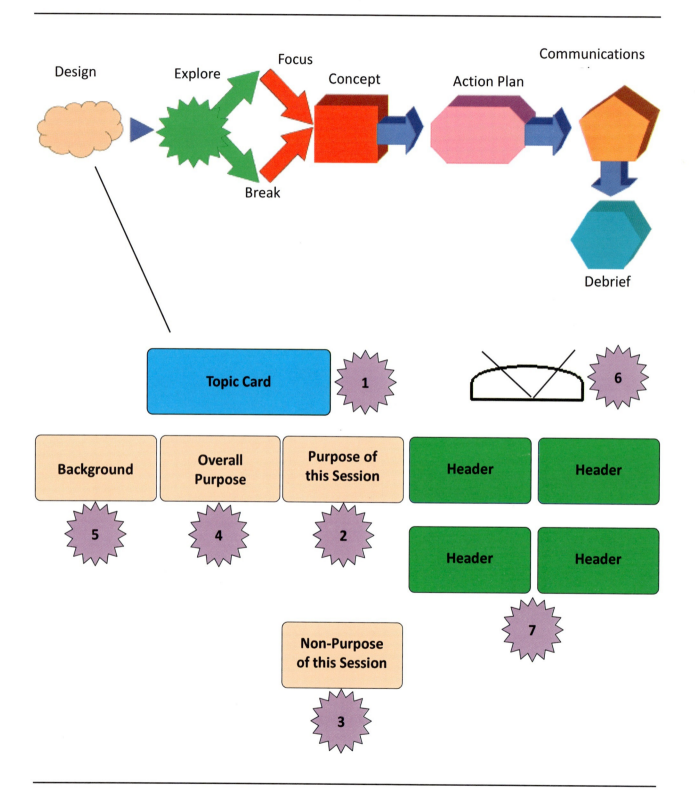

Design - *Design Template* 15

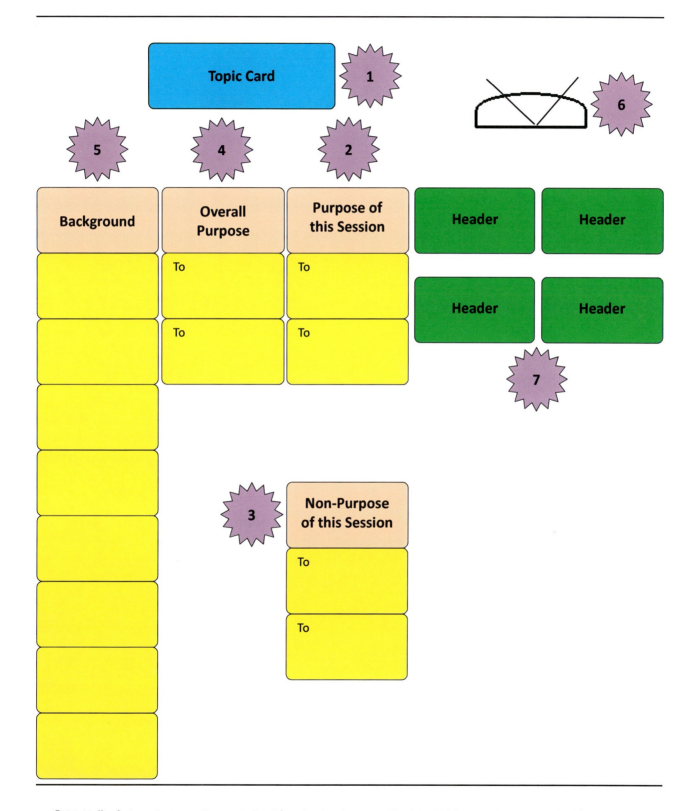

Topic Card

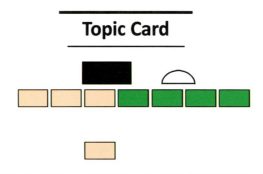

What it is
- The up-front issue/Topic the group will address

Why we use it
- It focuses participants' thinking

Hints
- Often begins with verbs ending in "-ing"
- Generally is 10 words or less
- May read like a book title
- Frequently requires reworking several times

Examples of weak Topic Cards
1. "Bonus Program"
2. "Set up an Advisory Board"

Examples of strong Topic Cards
1. "Introducing New Bonus Program to Canadian Managers"
2. "Developing a Major Dealer Advisory Board"
3. "Helping our Franchisee Hotels reduce operating costs"
4. "Focusing our Strategic Plan for the Next Two Years at a Tactical Level"
5. "Creating an Environment of Continuous Improvement as we work together as a team under one roof to serve our customers."

Quick Reference Examples
PAGES 16, 35, 39, 45, 112, 114, 116

Purpose of this Session

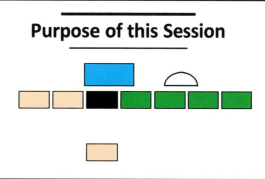

What it is
- Defines the results and deliverables of a specific session

Why we use it
- Helps participants know what they are to do
- Assists in recruiting the Project Team
- Energizes the group/drives for action
- Enables the group to manage time
- Helps participants know when they are finished

Hints
- Start with the word "To"
- Follow "To" with a verb
- Quantify, if possible, the desired outcome

Weak examples of Purpose of this Session
1. "To get ideas...as many as possible"
2. "To cut costs"
3. "Plan the introduction"

Strong examples of Purpose of this Session
1. "To generate 6 ideas we can do in the next 6 weeks"
2. "To determine 10 things we can do before the 3rd quarter'"
3. "To identify 'key' actions to be done in the next 30 days for the new product introduction"

Quick Reference Examples
PAGES   30, 35, 39, 45, 112, 114, 116

© McNellis & Associates • Compression Planning Institute • 724-847-2120 • www.compressionplanning.com

Non-Purpose of this Session

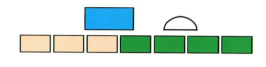

What it is
- It tells what is not included in the session
- It sets boundaries for content and / or behavior

Why we use it
- It keeps us from going off-track
- It helps us focus on the "real" issues
- It helps us manage group energy, thinking and time

Hints
- Start with the word "To"
- Follow "To" with a verb
- Avoid using "not" - it forms a double negative
- Think of the potential issues which could distract or disrupt the session
- Sort out what emotions and/or history could block progress

Weak examples of Non-Purpose of this Session
1. "To not reopen the union contract"
2. "History"

Strong examples of Non Purpose of this Session
1. "To reopen the union contract"
2. "To relive the history of this issue"

Quick Reference Examples
PAGES 19, 20, 30, 35, 39, 45, 112, 114, 116

Frequently the most useful part of design...the Non

Non-Purpose, Non-Market, Non-Service, Non-Product

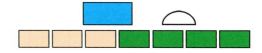

Definition of the NON - identifies what you don't want to achieve and helps you get a handle on what you actually need to accomplish.

The "Non-Purpose of this Session" always gets rave reviews in every training program we do. I get constant feedback about how helpful it is for getting groups focused and cutting wasteful side conversation that fritters away time and energy. It is such a simple but powerful tool that brings much more clarity to your group.

===

Hints when crafting your Non-Purpose(s):

1. You can use a Non for an Overall Purpose as well as a Non-Purpose for a Session. We don't teach this in the basic course because there is enough to focus on but it can help in more advanced and complex situations. You simply dig out what you don't want to accomplish overall in a project and it helps clarify the purpose. This ensures you have the broadest view possible when looking at your overall objectives.

   An example from something we were involved in once was a school district working to pass a bond levy. The Overall Purpose was: To get 1 more vote than the opposition. The Overall Non-Purpose was: To energize the opposition.

   Several past efforts to pass a levy failed. Because of the Non-Purpose they pursued ideas quietly and lulled the opposition into little effort because they thought the pro-levy groups weren't well organized or active. The pro-bond issue group worked "almost clandestinely" so as not to arouse the anti-bond issue people. It worked.

   Think of how many groups (with get out the vote measures) would have turned out the opposition as well as their own backers. I believe having such NON purpose clarity must have had some impact on the approach that ultimately passed the bond levy.

2. In a "Non-Purpose of this Session" you can use it in two basic ways.

   They are as follows:

   a. Content examples:
      - To deal with distribution issues
      - To deal with market trends in this session
      - To explore ideas outside our first stage charter

   b. Behavioral examples
      - To dwell in the past
      - To tell "war stories"

3. Do not force Non-Purposes in your design stage. If they naturally arise, great. Remember, you can add to them during the sessions whenever they pop up in discussion. Don't be surprised if you have more Non-Purposes than Purposes for this Session. It happens frequently, especially in strategic work sessions.

4. A Non-Purpose for this Session could very well turn into a Specific Purpose of this Session at a later date. These are typically content driven cards although in some cases, they could be behavioral driven.

   There may be an appropriate time to share "war stories" as these can be tremendous learning opportunities for new hires and newer managers. A recent one we facilitated was around "war stories" in their client/customer service department and how managers expertly handled some fairly bizarre requests.

5. Determining your Non-Audience or Non-Market for your product or service helps you in getting a bead on your customer. And figuring out how to sell to your non-market gets you great ideas for your target, ideal audience.

   For example - I do not drink coffee or tea (hot or cold). By targeting people like me (if it is worth doing) you will come up with a potential new audience (or market) and that will also get you great ideas for your ideal target market as well.

6. The same thing is true by defining your Non-Services. What aren't you going to do? In this day of 100% service there are times that a tighter focus can help.

   Many years ago a friend asked me to facilitate a group of parents of teenage drug addicts. There were a lot of ideas that people had and I give them immense credit for putting all but one in the category of Non-Programs and Non-Services. Yes there were immense needs but they focused 100% on helping parents get their lives under control when they were ready to explode due to their pain, frustration and anger. Their Non-Purpose was "to do anything about the children." Their focus was "to be there to help the parents at their most critical moment of crisis."

   After the parents got themselves "together" they could then deal with their own kids.

7. The "Non" certainly doesn't mean being negative. It means being clear. The greater the clarity the greater the results.

   Try starting out a session with the following Non-headers:
   - What don't we want to accomplish in this project
   - What don't we want to provide as a service
   - What don't we see in our product line

Overall Purpose

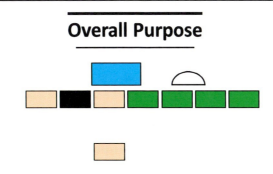

What it is
- The ultimate reason or context for addressing a particular issue, project, or opportunity
- The end product at the completion of the project or resolution of the issue or problem

Why we use it
- It focuses the group on what we really want to achieve
- It brings honesty to the session
- It provides a reference point for future sessions on this topic

Hints
- Start with the word "To" and follow it with a verb
- Quantify the outcomes by using "time", "$", "#'s"
- Convert your %'s to actual numbers - i.e. 10% represents 25 customers
- Ask "why" 5 times to drive towards the true purpose

Weak examples of Overall Purpose
1. "To be more helpful to our customers"
2. "To be well known"
3. "To get lots of involvement"

Strong examples of Overall Purpose
1. "To be absolutely indispensable to half of our customer base within 18 months"
2. "To be the supplier of choice by 7 of 10 players in the market"
3. "To get 20 managers spending 8 hours a month on client sites'"

Quick Reference Examples
PAGES 30, 35, 39, 45, 112, 114, 116

Background

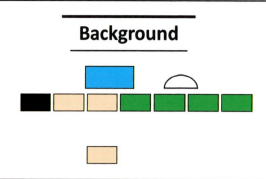

What it is
- A presentation of the critical and factual information on the topic necessary to clarify the purpose of the session

Why we use it
- It presents the necessary information for participating in this particular session
- It quickly brings the project team up to speed
- It keeps the group away from debating givens

Hints
- Limit it to 10 to 12 factual bits of information (Level I Background = Fact, Level II = Opinion)
- Design for the project team and for the Purpose of This Session
- Use symbols - # % ? <> $$
- Include: pictures, drawings, artifacts, samples, graphs, actual products or prototypes
- A timeline / flow chart may be helpful

Weak examples of Background data
1. "The engineers hate the software"
2. "ADG, API, CSA involved"
3. "Employees hate work"
4. "It's always been a problem"

Strong examples of Background data
1. "Engineers don't like the software because it's slow and unreliable"
2. "Account Data General, American Programs Inc., and Computer Software Association are partners in the venture"
3. "3 surveys completed during the last 5 years conclude employees are dissatisfied with employment at this company"
4. "The problem first surfaced in 1989 shortly after the consolidation of the two business units"

Quick Reference Examples
PAGES   30, 35, 39, 45, 112, 114, 116

Permission Meter

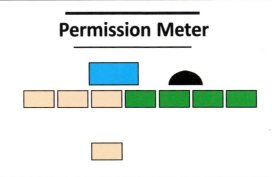

What it is
- A gauge of the desired level of thinking by the group
- An expectation setter

Why we use it
- It forces people to identify the needs/boundaries they are prepared to penetrate
- It clarifies the degree of freedom the group has for its session

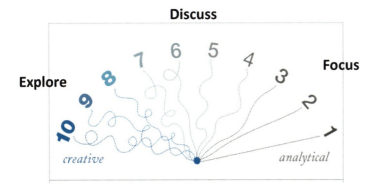

Hints
- Use with the client privately first
- Clients set the Permission Meter
- If it is not useful, do not use it
- Do not equate to risk

Quick Reference Examples
PAGES 30, 35, 39, 45, 113, 115, 117

Headers

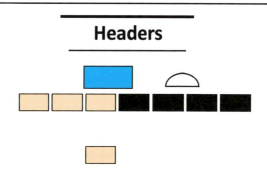

What they are
- Key components/???'s/issues to be addressed during the session
- Pathways to accomplishing the Purpose(s)

Why we use them
- They create categories to make the issue manageable
- They create energy and focus
- They solicit participation

Hints
- Listen to the client as you design
- Study the Background and Purposes
- List key ???'s or parts of the problem to surface Headers
- Think through all the process steps
- Develop 3-5 Headers
- State them in ???'s
- Use strong action verbs and rich language
- Sequence/stage the headers
- Use a MISC. Header to eliminate debates

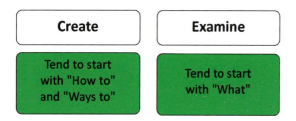

Quick Reference Examples
PAGES 30, 35, 39, 40, 45, 46, 47, 48, 49, 50, 51, 52, 53, 54, 55, 56, 57, 58, 59, 60, 61, 62, 63, 64, 69, 112, 114, 116

Design - *Boundary Questions*

TOPIC	1. What is the issue you want addressed? 2. What is the problem, opportunity or predicament that you face? 3. If you were to describe your issue to me in one sentence, it would be….. 4. What is the one single thing you must resolve?
OVERALL PURPOSE	1. What is the larger picture of this project? 2. How can you quantify this project in time, dollars or numbers? 3. If you can't directly measure where you want to be, how can you verify when progress is being made and the results happen? 4. What do you want to have accomplished when you are done? Specifically? In general terms?
PURPOSE OF THIS SESSION	1. When the session is over, what do you want available to you? 2. What are your expectations for this session? 3. How can you quantify your expectations in time, dollars or verifiables? 4. How can we assure the session is productive for you? 5. What do you need to walk away with...specifically?
NON-PURPOSE OF THIS SESSION	1. What could derail this session? 2. What should we not talk about? 3. What would be a waste of time to spend any effort on? 4. What is outside the boundaries of this topic? 5. Where are the landmines that can upset this topic?
PERMISSION METER	1. How welcome are participants to challenge the assumptions about this topic? 2. How much freedom does the group have to go down fresh pathways? 3. On a scale of 1-10 with 10 being 100% fresh and bold ideas and 1 being totally and specifically analytical...what type of thinking do you want? 4. How open would you say you are to having your basic concept challenged?
BACK-GROUND	1. What is your role in this project? 2. What support do you have? 3. How did this project get started? 4. What financial support is available? 5. What has been done to date? 6. What could stop this project? 7. Why are you working on this project? 8. What will happen if you are successful? 9. What will happen if you fail; or partially succeed? 10. What are 10-12 key facts I need to know to help you? 11. What visuals do you have that will help us in the session - charts, graphs, products, photos, ads, anything visual that helps tell the story?
HEADERS	1. What questions do you want explored? 2. What needs to be part of our session? 3. Who are the stakeholders in this project and what would they want this team to consider? 4. If you could resolve one issue in this project, what would it be? 5. What are the 3-5 key questions that will crack open your issue 6. Be sure to use "ways to" to turn some of their what questions into creative ones (if needed).

© McNellis & Associates • Compression Planning Institute • 724-847-2120 • www.compressionplanning.com

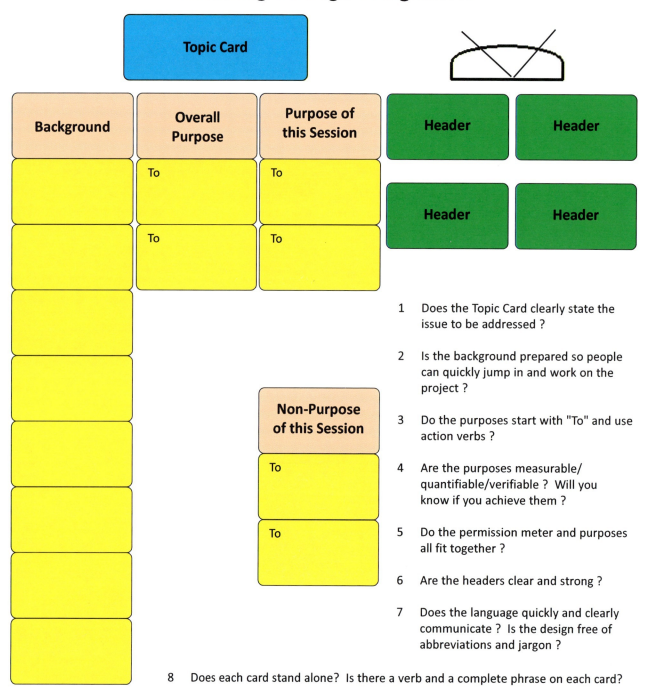

Design - Design Evaluation Form

Does the **Permission Meter** fit with your *Purposes*? ___yes ___no

[Topic Card]

[Background] [Overall Purpose] [Purpose of this Session] [Header] [Header]

Does the **Topic Card** start with a gerund (...ing)? ___yes ___no

Does the **Topic Card** clearly state the issue being addressed?
___ very clear ___possibly re-word

Is the Background prepared so people can jump in and work quickly?
___yes ___no

[Non-Purpose of this Session]

Do the Purposes all start with the word "to"?
- Overall Purpose ___yes ___no
- Purpose of this Session ___yes ___no
- Non-Purpose of this Session ___yes ___no

Are the Purposes measurable/quantifiable/verifiable"?
- Overall Purpose ___yes ___needs looked at
- Purpose of this Session ___yes ___needs looked at
- Non-Purpose of this Session ___yes ___needs looked at

Does the Language quickly and clearly communicate?
___yes ___needs attention

Additional Comments:

Is the Design free of abbreviations and jargon? ___yes ___be careful (see below)
- Background ___yes ___needs attention
- Overall Purpose ___yes ___needs attention
- Non-Purpose of this Session ___yes ___needs attention
- Purpose of this Session ___yes ___needs attention
- Headers ___yes ___needs attention

Does each Card stand alone? Has a verb with a complete phrase?
- Background ___yes ___needs attention
- Overall Purpose ___yes ___needs attention
- Non-Purpose of this Session ___yes ___needs attention
- Purpose of this Session ___yes ___needs attention
- Headers ___yes ___needs attention

Can the Design be strengthened by additional Artifacts?
___yes ___probably ___not sure

© McNellis & Associates • Compression Planning Institute • 724-847-2120 • www.compressionplanning.com

Design - *Action Verbs*

Activate	Cut	Formulate	Minimize	Select
Add	Connect	Fix	Move	Sell
Adjust	Create	Get	Meet	Send
Analyze	Convert	Guide	Obtain	Set up
Arrange	Decline	Go	Operate	Shop for
Apply	Decrease	Hire	Open	Show
Ask	Deduct	Hold	Participate	Spend time
Assure	Delay	Identify	Pay	Start
Attract	Destroy	Illustrate	Photograph	Stop
Avoid	Determine	Isolate	Prepare	Store
	Develop	Increase	Put	Structure
		Indicate	Protect	Substitute
Become			Permit	Sign
Begin	Distribute			Synchronize
Borrow	Display	Initiate		
Build	Divide	Induct	Prevent	
Buy	Do	Incorporate	Produce	Secure
Block	Drop	Instruct	Purchase	Take
Call	Eliminate	Insure	Qualify	Teach
Carry	Enroll	Investigate	Raise	Train
Check	Establish	Join	Read	Turn
	Expand	Keep	Rent	Transmit
Change		Learn	Replace	Transform
Combine	Extend		Reduce	Test
Choose	Enclose	Locate		Upgrade
Complete	Examine	Limit	Remove	
Compute	Facilitate	Load	Receive	Use
Consider	File	List	Record	Withdraw
Contact	Filter	Maintain	Restrict	Work
Contribute	Finance	Make	Retain	Write
Copy	Find	Maximize	Reverse	

**Effective facilitators listen for VERBS
and make sure printers capture them.**

Design - *Design Form*

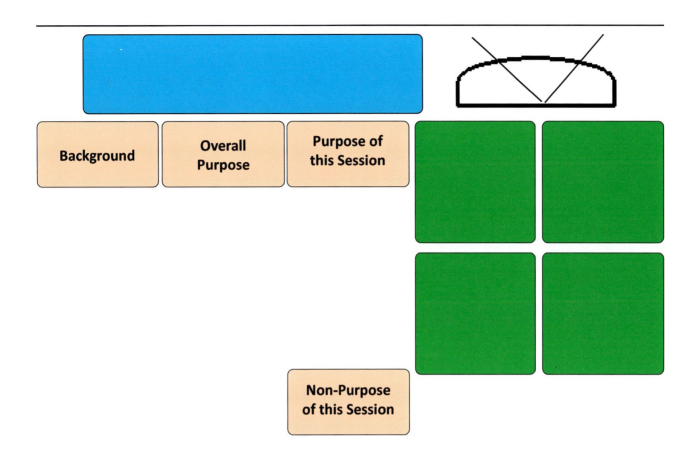

Client:_____

Session Date:_____

Time Frame of this Session:_____

Number of People In Session:_____

© McNellis & Associates • Compression Planning Institute • 724-847-2120 • www.compressionplanning.com

Models - Demonstration Model #1

Creating a Joint Academy for Highly Gifted Students

Background
- The Jones County Consortium for a Secondary School Academy for Gifted Students in the county operates from a $15,000 planning grant that was written by Kathy Wilson
- In 2/96 four county districts began collaboration on this project - Polk, Hamer, East Fork and Dow
- Dow is the administrative district for the project
- Support for the planning project was secured from all districts before the proposal was submitted
- District administrators & boards pledged their support
- Parent Councils in all districts have agreed to be involved

Overall Purpose
- To create an academy by September 1997 to meet the needs of at least 100 highly able students as defined by students' needs assessments
- A steering committee and 5 sub-committees have been formed to do the work
- A curriculum consultant has been retained
- A large community meeting was held to gain input
- We have six months to get a plan completed

Purpose of this Session
- A. To identify the most critical goals that will drive creation of a stand out academy
- B. To select 3 non-traditional approaches in creating the academy

Non-Purpose of this Session
- To debate the need for the Academy - it's a go
- To act as advocates for our own special interests or students
- To discuss where the academy will be headquartered
- To discuss criteria for admission
- To explore potential teachers

HEADERS

A.
- After the first year, what will we have accomplished?
- The learning outcomes students would never get in current schools
- For the year 2005 student, what must the academy have achieved?
- Why does the academy really exist?

B.
- Ways to make the academy a national model
- How can we make our academy "one of a kind?"
- Approaches which will WOW college recruiters
- MISC.

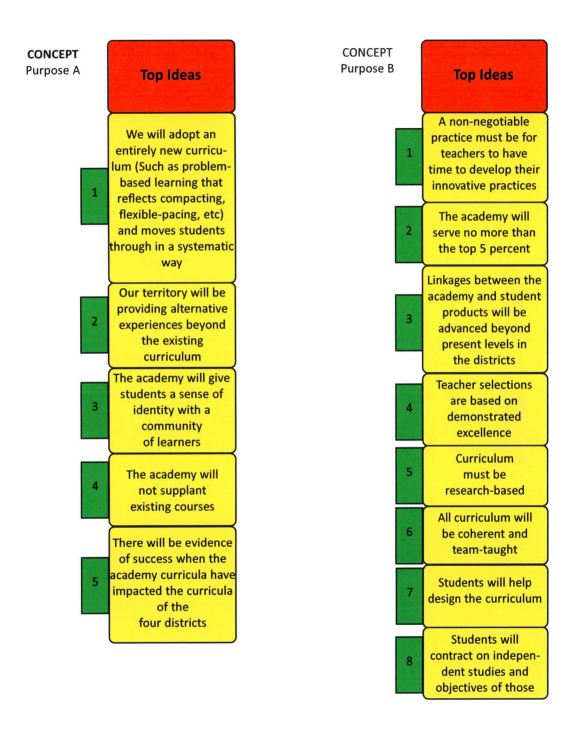

Models - *Demonstration Model #1*

PURPOSE A

ITEM:	Tasks	Who will do it	Deadline
We will provide alternative experiences beyond our existing curriculum	Identify types of alternative experiences than can be used	Joe, Susan, Bill	September 1
	Identify & benchmark districts that have strong AE	Hemm Henson	September 1
	Check legal issues around AEs identified	Mr. Smith (school board attorney)	September 30
ITEM: We will adopt an entirely new curriculum that reflects compacting, flexible pacing, etc. so the students can move through systematically	Inventory, investigate any additional resource needs	Jack, facilities team	October 15
	Identify parts of the current curriculum we can retain	Sarah, curriculum sub-group	September 15
	Identify missing parts curriculum where we need to fill	Sarah, curriculum sub-group	September 25
	See what state requirements we need to follow	Roger Dow	October 15

PURPOSE B

ITEM:	Tasks	Who will do it	Deadline
Teachers will be assured of ample time to develop their best, most innovative practices	Check teacher contract for language, requirements around time	Mr. Smith & Jim Slade (teacher assoc. rep)	October 1
	Determine impact on staffing if up to 20%	Sarah, curriculum sub-group	October 15

© McNellis & Associates • Compression Planning Institute • 724-847-2120 • www.compressionplanning.com

Models - *Demonstration Model #1*

Specific Messages

1. Legal issues must be researched
2. State regulations must be researched
3. Contract language on time, schedule has to be checked
4. Tasks, deadlines for Action Plan
5. Copy of this session report
6. Update on total project progress
7. Curriculum changes are planned
8. 20% planning time for faculty under consideration

Who needs to know	What they need to know	How will we tell them	Who Will Tell Them/ Deadline
Joe Jackson	4, 7	Memo	Sally W. - 8/15
Susan Harvey	4, 7	Memo	Sally W. - 8/15
Bill Winter	4, 7	Memo	Sally W. - 8/10
Mr. Smith	1, 3, 4	Letter	Harry P. - 8/20
Herm Henson	4, 7	E-mail	Walt Jones - 8/15
Jack Williams	5, 7	Face-to-face	Sally W. - 8/18
Sarah Lowe	2, 4, 5, 7	Face-to-face with written report	Jen A. - 8/20
Roger Dow	2, 4, 7	E-mail	Jen A. - 8/20
Bill Henry	1, 3, 4, 5, 8	Written report	Harry - 8/18
Curriculum sub-group	2, 4, 7	Meeting, writing	Sarah - 8/20
Principals	All	Written report	Sam J. - 8/20
Jim Slade	All	Writing, meeting	Sam J. - 8/15
Faculty reps	1, 2, 3, 4, 7, 8	Meeting, writing	Jim S. - 8/20
Supts./Boards	All	Meeting, writing	Sam - bd. meeting

© McNellis & Associates • Compression Planning Institute • 724-847-2120 • www.compressionplanning.com

Models - *Demonstration Model #1*

What went well?

- The "right" teachers were there
- We got a lot done in a short period of time
- Using the reminder balls
- Ron's prep work
- Ron's facilitation
- The room set-up
- Lots of good ideas
- We worked well as a team

How can we improve our next session?

- Get some parents here
- Have some ideas from the student council
- Meet first thing in the morning
- We need to watch speeches, judging

Lessons Learned

- We really can make some neat improvements
- REI is not a "crock"
- The value of preparation

© McNellis & Associates • Compression Planning Institute • 724-847-2120 • www.compressionplanning.com

Models - *Demonstration Model #2*

Planning our district's REI Phase I Action Plan

Permission Meter

Background
- REI is the Regular Education Initiative
- The state board trains on what REI is, is not
- All our teachers need to know more about REI
- REI and inclusion are not the same thing
- Districts will be required to complete an REI plan in the future
- We need an action plan to move ahead with implementation
- Our district excels in: Gifted, Special Ed, Alternative Ed, Vocational Ed
- Many parents of "regular" students feel kids are deprived

Overall Purpose
- To implement the first step of the REI plan by August 1996
- To strengthen programs for "regular" students so parents are pleased with plan overall by end of 1996-1997 school year

Purpose of this Session
- To identify 8-10 improvements in the Regular Education program in our high school

Non-Purpose of this Session
- To argue the need for REI
- To worry about the possible impacts on staffing/schedules
- To focus on dollars
- To discuss people, parents or students

(Categories)
- New courses which we need to add to curriculum to better serve "regular" kids
- How to modify teaching assignments and staff configurations to help "regular students"
- Ways to tap into different learning styles of students
- What would (parents, students, community leaders and the board) say we need to do
- Misc.

© McNellis & Associates • Compression Planning Institute • 724-847-2120 • www.compressionplanning.com

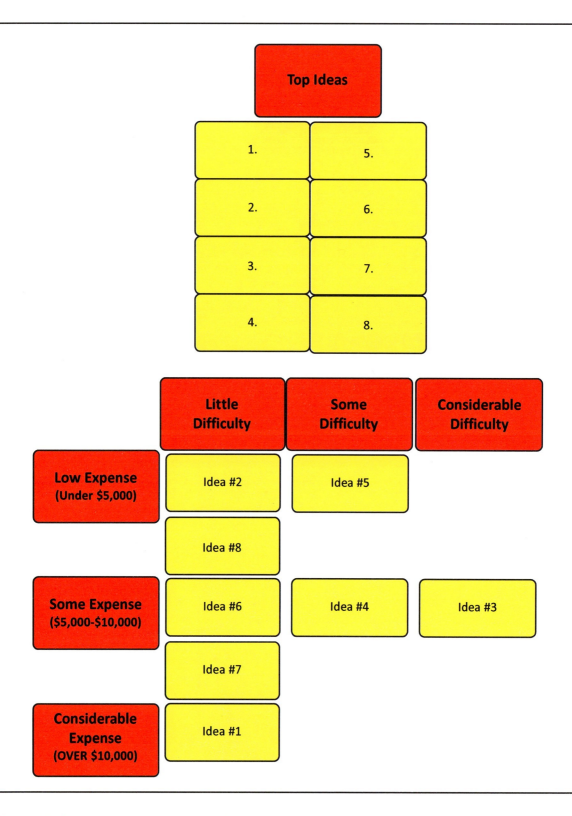

1 Month Action Plan

Tasks	Who will do it	Deadlines
Write summary of meeting	Paula	February 28
Prepare presentation to the PTA	Janet	March 8
Facilitate discussion at PTA	Tim	March 8
Incorporate parents input into the plan	Sue	March 10
Estimate training needs to incorporate changes	Jay	March 15
Estimate dollars needed to incorporate changes	Niki	March 17
Presentation of modifications for 96-97 to committee	Sue, with Bill and Jane	March 21

Models - Demonstration Model #2

Specific Messages:

1. There are changes coming in program
2. We will be giving input
3. Copies of the plan
4. Article on REI goals, outcomes
5. Process, timetable
6. Recommendations

Who needs to know	What they need to know	How will we tell them	Who will tell them/ Deadline
Current teachers & new teachers	1-5	Written report	Hope - 3/1
Parents	2, 5	Writing	Hope - 3/5
District-wide committee	5, 6	Writing, in person	Bob - 3/15

© McNellis & Associates • Compression Planning Institute • 724-847-2120 • www.compressionplanning.com

Designing the first phase of a water park

Permission Meter

Background
- Water park to be built on the site of an old steel mill plant
- One mile of river front property
- This is a 2 phase project
- Phase 1 - day use only / Phase 2 - night use
- Capacity is 3000 visitors per day
- Approximate cost of Phase 1 is $3M
- After property closing, have 7 months to build

Overall Purpose
- To design the first phase of a waterpark that can be built in 7 months
- To show a profit in 5 years

Purpose of this Session
- To generate 2-3 ideas each for:
  - A. Water slide design
  - B. Food service
  - C. Extra attractions
- To select one idea each for implementation

Non-Purpose of this Session
- To discuss phase 2 of this project
- To debate the 7 month time frame

Waterslide designs the public will never stop talking about
- Develop 2 slides - single person and two person
- Build the tallest slide in the country - 12 stories high
- Create a 1/3 mile lazy river for tubes
- Build gradual mini slides for the kiddie pool
- Install a slide which is one block long
- Design a slide which ends in free fall
- Build a slide which is totally enclosed like a dark hold
- Make slides like pretzels
- Try a long slide with a 115 degree drop

© McNellis & Associates • Compression Planning Institute • 724-847-2120 • www.compressionplanning.com

Models - *Demonstration Model #3*

How can we do food on the board-walk in a smart, efficient way?

- Locate all food vendors in the same area
- Display different "fronts" to create the illusion of different stores
- Create an international food theme - "fronts" show country and theme
- Build one preparation area for all fronts
- Establish one storage area, one refrigeration area to serve all food areas
- Purchase food jointly to lower costs, volume discounts

Low cost extras that will add fun to the beach

- Design a frisbee golf course - have a par 3
- Have a treasure hunt for free give aways
- Build a competition grade sand volleyball court
- Challenge the lifeguards to volleyball for free admission
- Hold sandcastle making competition
- Have bathing suit fashion shows
- Provide sculling activities on the river
- Plan dancing on the beach every day at 3:00 for all ages
- Build a fishing pool for preschoolers

Misc.

- Install washers and dryers for guests
- Provide dryers in shower areas
- Offer on-site photo developing

© McNellis & Associates • Compression Planning Institute • 724-847-2120 • www.compressionplanning.com

Models - *Demonstration Model #3* 41

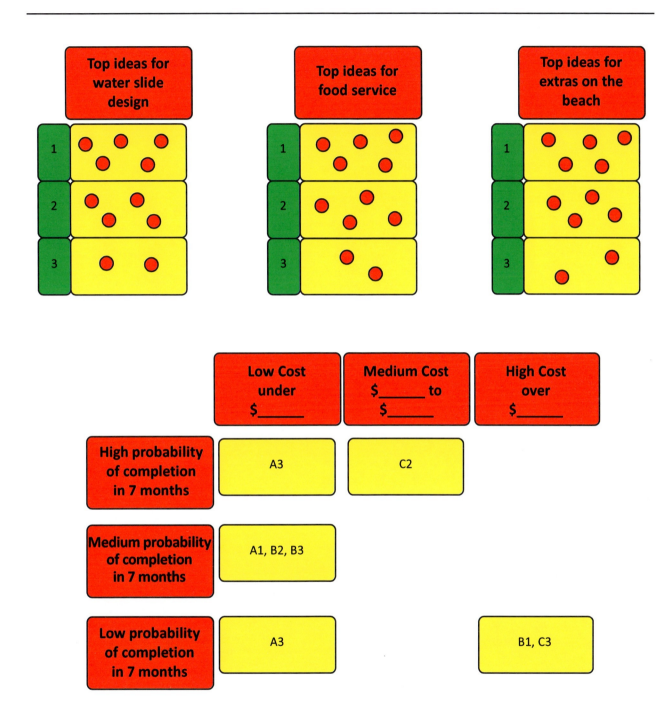

Tasks	Who will do it	Deadline
Prepare master design with landscape architect	Conrad	November 1
Begin grading of area	Bob	November 1
Finalize contract with slide company	Conrad	December 1
Design food service area	Matt	February 15
Select company for employee uniforms	Alisa	March 2

Specific Messages	Who needs to know	What they need to know	Who will tell them	How will we tell them/ Deadline
	Our attorney	1	Hanna	Phone call & letter - 11/1
1. Update on which contracts are finalized	Landscape architect	2, 4	Conrad	In Person - 11/3
2. Summarize findings on site visit	Waterslide company	3	Paula	Phone Call & Letter - 11/5
3. Announce specifications on slides	State dept. of transportation for signs	2, 5	Walt	Phone call & presentation - 11/12
4. Date of project manager's meeting	Water and power companies	2, 5	Walt	Memo or letter - 11/20
5. Progress on food vendors	Food suppliers	3	Hanna	Formal presentation - 12/3

Models - Demonstration Model #3

What went well
- We kept to our schedule
- We had great ideas
- Visiting the site
- Everyone stayed until the end
- We're walking out with an Action Plan
- Everyone printed and pinned
- Several people facilitated
- The process worked

How can we improve our next session
- Strive for a more diverse team
- Start earlier so we can end earlier
- Use balls to control speeches
- Allow more time for the action plan
- Arrange for more hearty snack in the afternoon

Lessons Learned
- Everyone has something to contribute
- You don't have to be an expert to contribute
- It pays to build on ideas
- A session design helps us stay on track
- Suspending judgment is difficult

© McNellis & Associates • Compression Planning Institute • 724-847-2120 • www.compressionplanning.com

Models - *Demonstration Model #4*

Creating a National Center of Excellence for Advanced Technological Education

Permission Meter

Background

- Deadline for preliminary proposal: 11/1/1993
- Deadline for final proposal: Spring 1994
- This is a new program - there are no existing models
- We are forging new ground - we must innovate
- Must involve community college, university, business and high schools
- Approximate cost of Phase 1 is $3M
- Must focus on technology education - not engineering
- The Sinclair/University of Dayton partnership is very strong

Overall Purpose

- To write a successful proposal to NSF/ATE
- The preliminary proposal is only 10 pages - no details needed
- See summary of NSF RFP White Paper
- The Advanced Integrated Manufacturing Center planning is aligned with the RFP

Purpose of this Session

1. To decide upon the proposal type
2. To determine 3-5 ideas for the following aspects of the proposal:
   A. Structure
   B. Service Area
   C. Focus
   D. Clients
   E. Services
3. To plan the proposal development process

Non-Purpose of this Session

- To worry about the details since this is a preliminary proposal

What type of preliminary proposal shall we submit?

- Go for the gusto: National Center grant (5 year, $1 million per year)
- Planning grant
- Project grant

© McNellis & Associates • Compression Planning Institute • 724-847-2120 • www.compressionplanning.com

Models - Demonstration Model #4

What is the focus of the NSF/ATE Prepoposal?

- Primary Partners: University of Dayton, Advanced Integrated Manufacturing (AIM), local tooling and maching industry, General Motors
- Create an Advisory Council of local manufacturers
- Business and Industry role - use for DACUM; focus groups, reactions to ideas; resources (time, equipment)
- Other Partners: Dayton Public Schools, Montgomery County Public Schools, Miami-Valley Tech.Prep Consortium, Dayton Affiliate Societies Council
- Diagram partnership with the AIM Center in the middle

What structure for the proposal?

- Sinclair is fiscal agent
- Advanced Integrated Manufacturing Center submits proposal on behalf of Sinclair and the University of Dayton
- AIM Center may need a federal ID number
- The University of Dayton will be a subcontractor

What is our service area?

- Year 1 - Developmental Phase - local activity
- Years 2-4 - Pilot Phase - Regional Activity (Midwest)
- Year 5 - Roll Out Phase - National Activity

© McNellis & Associates • Compression Planning Institute • 724-847-2120 • www.compressionplanning.com

Models - *Demonstration Model #4*

Who are our clients?

Primary Clients: College Faculty, Program Administrators, High School Faculty

Secondary Clients: Employers, Parents, Traditional Students, Non-traditional students, Special outreach to special populations

What services will we provide our clients?

- Curricula for: high school, community college, universities
- Curriculum materials such as textbooks, AV, etc.
- Faculty development in-service opportunities, such as summer institutes
- Laboratory enhancements will be requested (hardware and software)
- Hands on opportunities for learning
- Faculty development programs
- Implementation plan for other colleges
- We will be a prototype laboratory model - a lab school
- National clearninghouse for related curricula materials
- Opportunities and methods for coop, apprenticeships, and research assistants
- Electronic networks for faculty development
- Faculty exchange loan programs to industry
- Publicity, outreach will be required
- Articulation agreements (high school, community college, university

Who are our competitors?

- Milwaukee Area Technical College
- Grand Rapids/ Ferris State
- University of Toledo, Com. Tech, Owens Tech.
- Monroe Community College (MI)
- Cuyahoga Community College

© McNellis & Associates • Compression Planning Institute • 724-847-2120 • www.compressionplanning.com

Headers - *Examples*

Provocative Headers

- How can we blast the socks off our competition
- How can we turn our ___ from careless to caring
- How can we make every worker feel like royalty
- Ways to be indispensable to our customers
- How can we make people clamor for our services
- What will grab the attention of every employee
- What can we do that is so special our employees will tell everyone about it
- How can we get people fired up about this opportunity
- If you had a magic wand, what would you change
- If this product could speak, what would it say

Marketing

- Non-traditional ways to advertise
- Ways to make our competition irrelevant
- What is our unique service?
- What do our customers expect?
- Who are our prime prospects?
- Where do we have a competitive advantage
- What are the rules about packaging
- New product/service ideas
- Ways to build repeat customers
- How can we make our price more attractive
- Ways to blow the socks off our customers
- Ways to do more business per sale
- New ways to obtain business
- Ways to attract new customers
- Key phrases that will grab our customers
- Cutting edge advertising & promotion ideas we can use
- How can we attract publicity

Headers - *Examples*

General Situations	Who is our Market	Who is our Non-Market	Special products/ services we offer
What are we selling	What resources can we tap	What are alternative approaches	Potential hang-ups
Good examples to study	Bad examples to study	What are the timing issues	What are our concerns
What are our incentives for customers	What are our incentives for our employees	How do we make it interesting	How do we make it indispensable
Ways to monitor our progress	Non-traditional things we can do	Our niche could be.....	Things we can do no one else is doing
Ways to make alternate approaches work for us	Ways to activate ideas hanging around	What are the legal issues	What other industries have similar products/services
Premises we are working under	Who is our competition	"Catchy Phrases"	Ways to tap into resources

© McNellis & Associates • Compression Planning Institute • 724-847-2120 • www.compressionplanning.com

tips and tricks   **21**   *The McNellis Company Compression Planning®*

"Surfacing Great Headers"

You know the old saying "Don't reinvent the wheel?" Well, headers are like that. Many great headers can be found in written materials like magazines, journals, and books! There are many great sources of questions that can be adapted to any situation! Use your imagination, get creative, and ADAPT!

One of the most interesting books we've read lately was written by Jay Abraham and entitled <u>Getting Everything You Can Out Of All You've Got - 21 Ways You Can Out-Think, Out-Perform, and Out-Earn the Competition</u>. Here's how you can take a book and identify and surface headers.

These headers were created by studying the outline of the book's text. A you read, you'll find that headers will jump out at you. Try it with a book you like.

Your Flight Plan

Ways we limit our business by doing the same thing our competitors do	Ways to position our product/service as having a unique benefit they don't receive from competitors	Ways to incorporate our unique advantage or benefit into everything we say and do	What are the elements of a totally risk-free offer we can make?
They stopped buying temporarily and just never get around to dealing with us again - how do we regain their business?	Ways to energize them to do business with us again	What do we want to track?	Ways to get new opportunities in their changed circumstances
Unconventionally fresh, superior, or exciting ways of doing _____	Breakthrough ways to transform our product/service from a commodity into a prized proprietary item/relationship	Breakthrough ideas to reinvent our business before some competitor does it to us	Where's the BIG OVERLOOKED opportunity here?

© McNellis & Associates • Compression Planning Institute • 724-847-2120 • www.compressionplanning.com

Your Business Soul - The Strategy of Preeminence

As you read a chapter, note with a red pen any questions that jump out at you

- Ways we need to change how we think about, deal with and speak to our clients
- Ways to get new opportunities in their changed circumstances
- Ways to convert from a "we" to a YOU orientation
- Ways to contribute, acknowledge and assure our clients that we care about them

Choose a book pertaining to your issue at hand!

Make 'em an Offer They Can't Refuse

- Ways to TOTALLY and COMPLETELY guarantee the purchase for our clients
- Ways to eliminate the purchasing risk for our clients
- Ways to help people decide to act today - immediately and without fear or concern
- What "specific" elements of our guarantee can we offer?

Would You Like the Left Shoe, Too?

- Ways we actually limit the amount of business people do with us
- Basic services or related products we can add to a sale
- What combinations of products and services can we offer?
- Ways to increase the size or frequency of purchase
- Ways to turn one-shot purchases into ongoing purchases
- Fresh ways to package current products and services
- Ways to take haphazard and erratic customers and make them regular customers
- What products and services can I reposition to an upscale market?

© McNellis & Associates • Compression Planning Institute • 724-847-2120 • www.compressionplanning.com

PROVOCATIVE HEADERS

January brings us another 31 headers from Jay Abraham's book entitled <u>Getting Everything You Can Out Of All You've Got - 21 Ways You Can Out-Think, Out-Perform, and Out-Earn the Competition</u>. Here are a few McNellis hints on how you might want to use these headers:

1.	Tie them to your purposes. If you are wrestling with topics on business development, see if you can use one or several of these headers to help unleash your group's energy and best thinking.

2.	If you like a grouping of headers, design a session and specific purpose that will be answered by the questions you choose. You can work backwards when doing a design as well. You may see a question or set of questions you know you should be addressing. With the questions in mind, simply reverse-design your session! Try it, it works!

Remember the Design Alert Service! Our facilitators and trainers are pros at drafting questions and are here to help you when YOU NEED IT! Take advantage of this free, lifelong service!

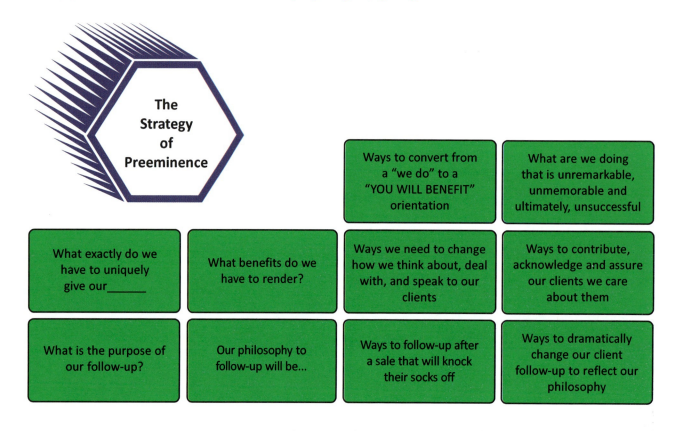

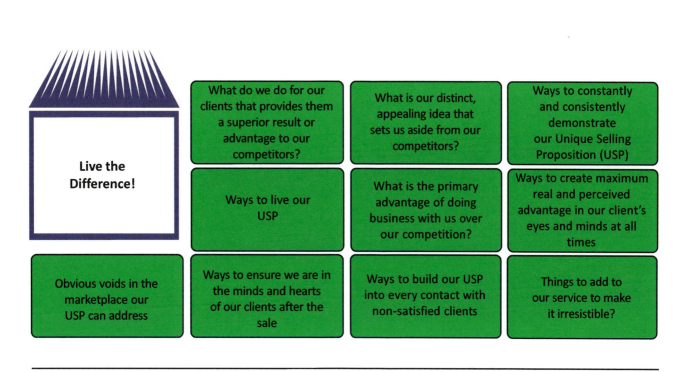

Headers - *Formations*

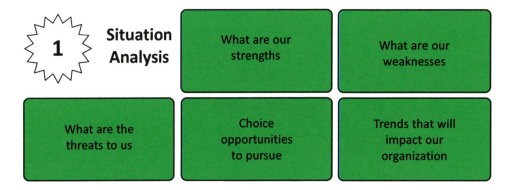

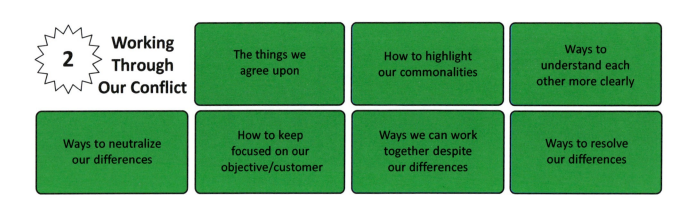

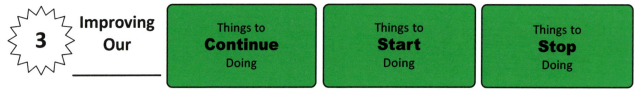

Use these headers in a left to right order (lowers defenses)

Examples
Improving our *Team*
Improving our *Planning Process*
Improving our *Order Fulfillment*
Improving our *Budgeting Process*

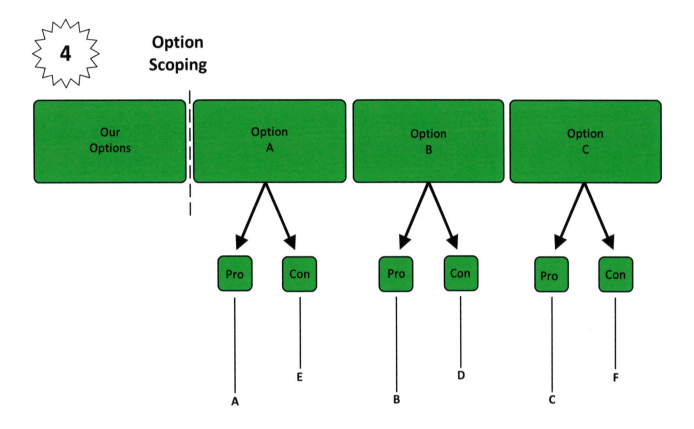

Topic Card Examples
- Assessing a piece of equipment
- Selecting a college
- Determining a strategy
- Designing site improvements

Note
1. List all possible options under the first header
2. Focus down to the top 2 or 3 options
3. Do all the pros, A, B & C
4. Take a break
5. Do all the cons, in a different order than the pros
6. Be open to new options emerging
7. Select the desired option

Headers - *Formations*

5 Co-Ordinating Activities/Teams

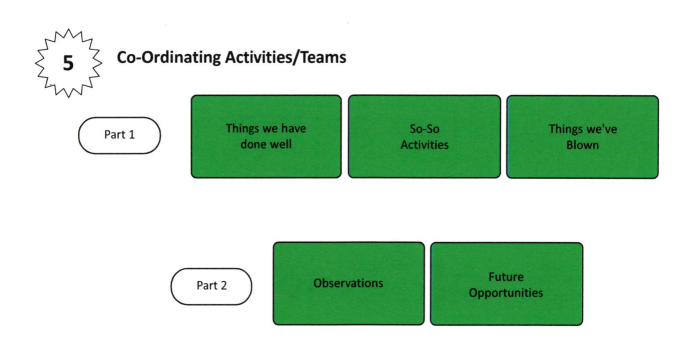

6 Statement of the problem

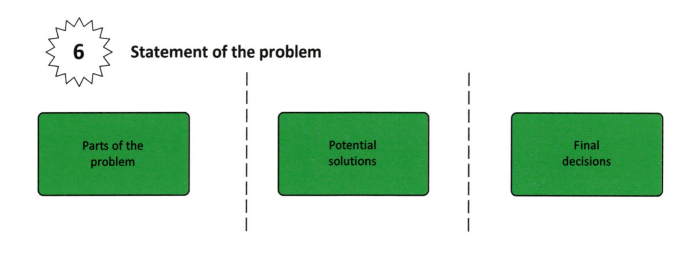

Headers - *Formations*

7 — Developing our Mission

	What are our aspirations	How will we be unique and different in five years	What have we dreamed about for the future
What do we want to be known for in the years to come	What will be our legacy to the next generation	What will inspire and excite stakeholders for years to come	What opportunities must we seize
What are trends to which we must be sensitive	What is the one thing we must never take our eyes off	As we look into the future, what do we want to significantly change	How must we fundamentally change how we do business
If we were starting our business tomorrow, how would we put it together	What new markets should we pursue	Where do we need to concentrate our efforts in the future	What new relationships should we explore

8 — Defining our Mission

Simply defined, what is our purpose	What is our special calling	What is the real reason we exist	What business(es) are we really in
What is our end product	Who do we serve	What is our special place/role in the marketplace	How do we differ from our competitors
How do our customers define our business	What is our niche	For what are we known	What is our territory

© McNellis & Associates • Compression Planning Institute • 724-847-2120 • www.compressionplanning.com

Supplemental Notes: The interrelationship between Mission, Vision, and Core Values

Our Mission Statement

- Tells us **WHY** we exist
- Provides reason and function
- Is **NOW** focused
- Is written with practical and concrete language
- Reflects current realities

Our Vision Statement

- Tells us **WHAT** we will become
- Points toward results and outcomes
- Is **FUTURE** oriented
- Uses language which may be ideal, imaginative, and/or metaphorical
- Reflects future realities

Our Core Values/Key Beliefs

- Tells us **HOW** we will act/behave
- Helps define the process
- Is **DYNAMIC** as we move into the future
- Incorporates language which is in behavioral terms
- Focuses upon our actions

Our Mission Statement is used to...

- Define who we are
- Explain what we are all about
- Define boundaries of our work
- Guide our future goal setting

Our Vision Statement is used to...

- Define the future
- Communicate our highest purpose
- Create a common identity
- Foster risk-taking and courage
- Inspire commitment
- Encourage creativity
- Provide energy and enthusiasm

Our Core Values/Key Beliefs are used to...

- Define the organizations:
  - Practices
  - Performance
  - Processes
  - People
- Make daily and key decisions
- Call for compliance

Determining Our Core Values and Key Beliefs

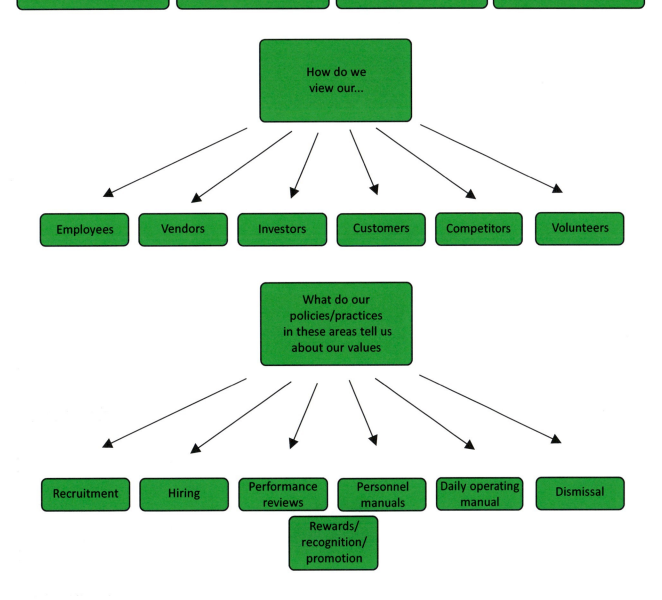

10 — Assessing Where We Are In The Quality Process

- What are the ?'s that pop into our minds on this issue
- Ways schedule and cost squeeze quality
- What are the executives doing to discourage quality
- What unpurposeful actions do we require of employees
- What are the thoughtless and unconcerned ways we deal with employees
- What daily procedures turn-off employees
- What are our company's norms of quality
- Ways non-conformance is costing us
- Where are our greatest opportunities for error
- How would our customers define quality
- How would our customers rate our quality
- Where are our most lucrative impacts for corrective action

11 — Committing the Executive Team to Action on Quality

- Ways to become educated on what is involved in genuine quality
- How to change our attitudes and actions
- Actions we will take to prove we are serious
- Ways to keep "egg off our face" while beginning this process
- Ways to keep this process from being meaningless & fruitless
- Ways to supply the where-with-all to every employee to meet the requirements
- What should our policy read like
- Ways to make "zero defects" a way of life
- What will be our specific requirements
- Ways to measure our standards

© McNellis & Associates • Compression Planning Institute • 724-847-2120 • www.compressionplanning.com

Building Quality Into Our Quality Improvement

- Ways to make our specific requirements understood by everyone
- Ways to keep this process from being cheapened & trivialized
- Ways to get every employee energized & committed to meet quality requirements
- Ways to keep the quality process hassle-free
- Ways to make tracking non-conformance a breeze
- Ways to prevent non-conformance
- Ways to encourage & help every employee to meet the requirements

Terry Idle's Product and Business Development

- What type of products could we sell in the mall
- How can we extend/expand what we are currently doing
- How can we improve our customer service to increase market share
- What stressors do our customers encounter with our current products/services
- How can we remold our present products for new applications
- Risky business ventures that could pay off
- How can we transfer our current "know how"
- No one else is as good as we are at _____
- How can we make our product more affordable
- How can we make our product appear more luxurious
- Products we can develop that will save labor
- Other uses for our current products
- How can we leap into the market
- Unseen markets/businesses we are not seeing for our current products
- Ways to involve our customers in developing new products

Training Applications using Storyboards

1. Use at the beginning of a training session to introduce the course agenda and show where on the agenda the participants' learning expectations will be met.

Board A

- What skills do you want to walk out with?
- What knowledge do you want to walk out with?

Board B

- Course Agenda
  - 8am
  - 9am
  - 10am

First, generate ideas under the headers on Board A.

Next, physically move the cards, one by one, on Board A to the corresponding agenda item on Board B. Give a verbal explanation as you do this.

If there are participant expectations which don't correspond with any part of your course agenda, acknowledge this and tell the participants whether or not you will modify the course to meet the expectations.

A modification of the above approach:
In a session on "Effective Presentations," ask participants to think of their most admired presenters/speakers. Then, on Board A, have them generate on cards all the characteristics of those effective presenters. Finally, physically move the cards on Board A to the corresponding agenda item on Board B, showing where on the agenda the desired presentation characteristics will be learned.

2. Use with a group of employees or managers to do a training needs assessment.

- What tasks are required in the job?
- What areas of competency are required in the job?
- What areas of expertise are required in the job?
- What skills will you (they) need in the future?

Facilitation Hints
Remind the participants to suspend judgment. You may want to try subdividing into small groups for part of the idea generation.

When idea generation is complete, dot. Instruct the participants to dot the 3-4 tasks they most want to perform more effectively, the areas of expertise and competencies they most want to improve, etc.

If there are different employee types or levels in the group, give each type/level a different color dot.

© McNellis & Associates • Compression Planning Institute • 724-847-2120 • www.compressionplanning.com

Headers - *Training Applications*

3. **Do a warm-up at the beginning or during a session.**

   [Ways to improve these chairs] [Ways to improve the food] [Unique ways to...]

4. **Use a storyboard as a visual aid to your presentation.**

   Select a concept which can be given a visual treatment. Cut cards of different colors into circles, squares, triangles, arrows, clouds, or any other suitable shapes. Then, print pertinent information on the cards. Arrange the cards on the board face down, turn the cards right side up and re-pin them as you progress through the verbal explanation of the concept.

5. **Use storyboards in inductive learning.**

   As part of a training session, present specific facts or examples to support a concept. Ask participants, in small groups, to derive general principles from these facts/examples, and to print the principles on cards. Comment on the derived principles as you pin the cards on the board.

   [Lessons learned from _____]

6. **Use storyboards to reinforce application of newly learned knowledge and skills.**

   At the end of a training session, ask participants to develop individual or group action plans which outline specific actions and deadlines for applying their new knowledge and skills.

   [Ways I will apply new knowledge and skills] [Deadline for demonstrating new skills]

7. **Use storyboards to design a new course.**

   [What is the Overall Goal of the course?] [What are the Terminal Objectives?] [What are the Modules or Critical Content pieces?]

   MODULE #1 (Select the course modules before moving on to the next headers)

   [Strategies for teaching this module] [Media/materials we will use] [Ways we'll evaluate learning] [Ways we'll provide practice]

Facilitation Hints (**Repeat Module #1 for all subsequent modules)
Work these headers in whatever order makes the most sense to you. Some folks prefer to start by deciding the critical content/modules. Next, they develop the overall goal and terminal objectives. Then they decide teaching strategies, media, etc. Others prefer to work the headers in the order given here.

© McNellis & Associates • Compression Planning Institute • 724-847-2120 • www.compressionplanning.com

8. **Use storyboards to debrief training sessions.**

   This is particularly beneficial when you are piloting a new course, or revising an existing one. You can debrief with all the participants or with a representative few. You can debrief during a session as well as at the end. You can debrief a portion of the course as well as the entire course. Or use a debriefing to get feedback on new instructional materials.

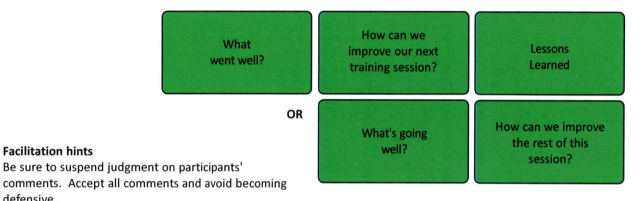

Facilitation hints
Be sure to suspend judgment on participants' comments. Accept all comments and avoid becoming defensive.

9. **Use a storyboard as a display board in a corner of the training room.**

   For example: Display examples of past successes. Or post photos of former classes. Display biographical information about the instructors. Pin competitors' products to the board or statistical data which support the need for this training program. Use color and make it visually appealing.

10. **Use storyboards to plan a meeting.**

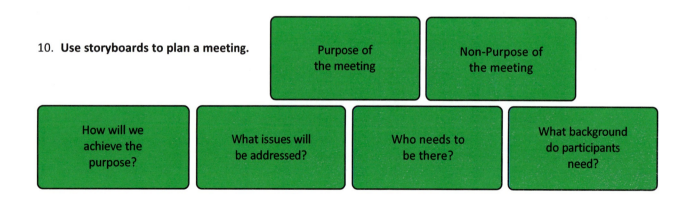

© McNellis & Associates • Compression Planning Institute • 724-847-2120 • www.compressionplanning.com

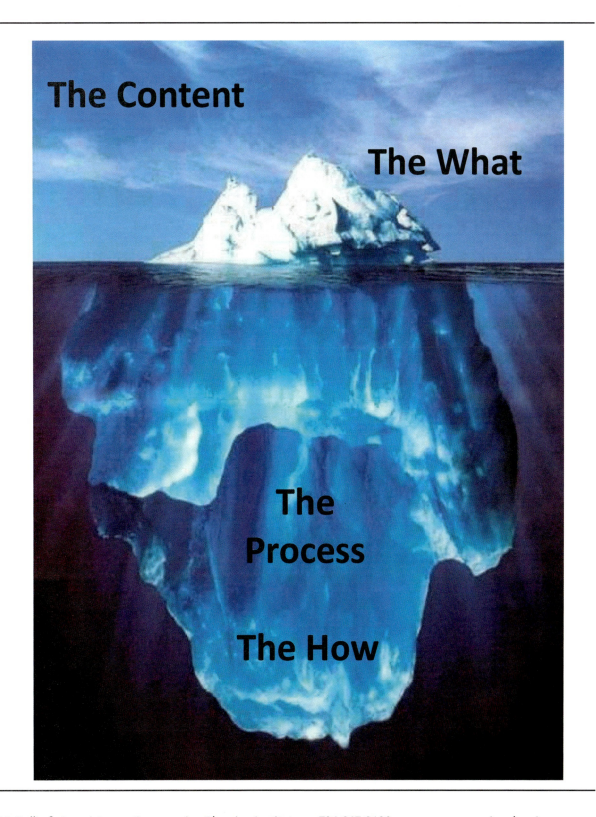

The Roles of the Facilitator throughout the Master Planning Model

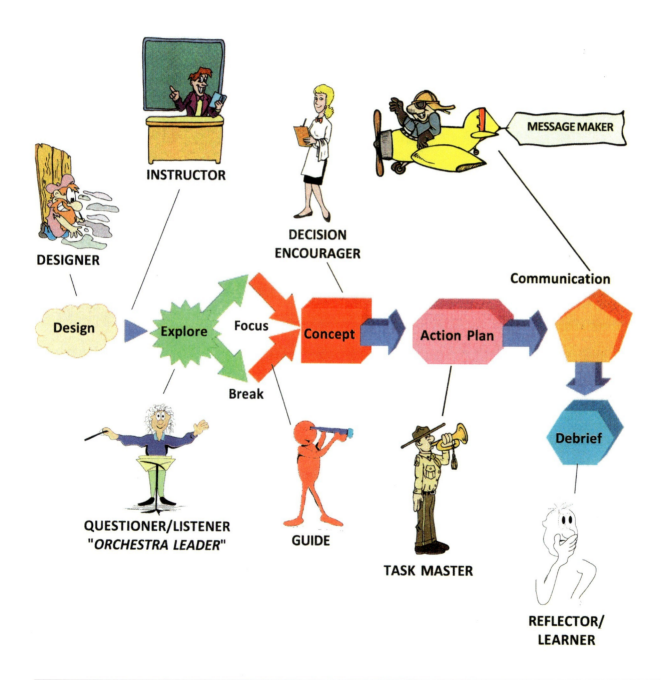

Tips and Techniques #1

1. **Stand**. You have better control of the group and you can see more of what's going on than if you sit.
2. Use your **arms** and **face** to encourage people and to draw them out.
3. **Step back** every few minutes to view the entire storyboard; avoid blocking the boards.
4. Be sure to explain and **post the guidelines** at the beginning of the session, especially in your early sessions.
5. **Protect** people and their ideas.
6. Do not get too serious too fast. Allow for **creativity** and **innovation** to happen. Make it comfortable for people to express **non-conventional** ideas, if that is what you are truly seeking.
7. **Capture all ideas**. Even if they seem goofy, make sure they're printed on a card and put on the storyboard. These are often ideas which can be spun into very workable concepts.
8. Concentrate on **remaining neutral**. Function as an orchestra leader, keeping an open and balanced flow of ideas. Facilitate the process, not the content.
9. Do not let people, especially the printers, get hung up on **spelling**.
10. Don't **play off the client** too much because it shuts down the team's contributions.
11. Keep in mind where you are in the **Master Planning Model**.
12. **Take down** headers that don't work.
13. **Keep a few headers handy** in case the process slows down...Put the headers up and see what happens.
14. When you **switch headers** - read them.
15. Periodically **check with the client** - "Are we getting what you need/want?"
16. Do not panic when things slow down. People need "**think time**." Allow some quiet while participants think.
17. Put the group on "hold" and use a "time-out" to discuss what is keeping the group from **working effectively**.
18. **Ask the group** for help if you don't know how to proceed.
19. Pull **diversions** back on track.
20. Get the group actively **spinning/churning** ideas.
21. Use "pro-active" **language** such as "let's try" or "how we can" rather than "should we" and "why not consider."
22. Avoid using "good idea" language - it is "**positive judgment**." Use neutral language like "yes" or "let's capture that."
23. Encourage people to **symbolize ideas**. Many times a simple drawing can illustrate a great deal of information.
24. Sometimes groups need time just to talk. Point this out and **protect the process**.
25. Be aware - remind participants of the **permission meter**.
26. Do not let the session go more than 90 minutes without a **break**.
27. Always **debrief** the session. Spend a few minutes discussing the process and how the team worked together.
28. **Do it...do it...do it!**

© McNellis & Associates • Compression Planning Institute • 724-847-2120 • www.compressionplanning.com

Neutral Facilitation

Role

- Develop the structure or process to help achieve the desired outcomes
- Manage the process during the session, watching the timing, flow and energy to keep the team on time and directed toward the purpose
- Ensure that team members share information, understand it and process it in an open, participative environment
- Protect the self-esteem of all participants

Characteristics

- Disengage from content - remain neutral
- Listen well and exhibit patience and sensitivity to people
- Tolerate ambiguity in order to work through complex issues that resist clear definition
- Know your own strengths and weaknesses and do not force them on the group
- Adapt your behavior and style to meet the group's needs and the sensitivity of the content

How to remain neutral when you're not

- Ask yourself privately what investment you have in the issue before you begin
- Make sure the group knows when you are facilitating and when you are participating. Say, "I'm stepping out of the facilitator role now," then give your idea
- Ask someone on the team to monitor your neutrality
- Provide a thorough, accurate and factual background
- Try making "suspended judgement" a way of life rather than an attribute you pull out only when facilitating a group

Ways to Keep the Session Moving

Quick & Easy

- Move to a new Header
- Symbolize it 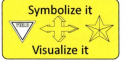 Visualize it
- Change Roles
- Take a Break
- Look back to: **Purposes** and **Background**
- Sub-divide the group
- Pause - Allow participants time to think
- Pick out 3 or 4 cards that have potential to be spun

Some Planning

- A ·)· B Change Perspective
- Do a Warm-up
- Think as an object or a process
- Immerse the group in artifacts

WORKING WITH LARGE GROUPS
(FROM 20 TO 100+ PARTICIPANTS)

Working with large groups can be quite rewarding. While large groups pull more energy out of us as facilitators, they are often very fun because of the group dynamics which transpire. Because of its diversity, generally, a large group provides richness of ideas which we can develop more fully.

To effectively work with large groups facilitators need to deliberately manage several dynamics in the group:
1. Energy
2. Time
3. Dominating and difficult people
4. Participation
5. Diverse perspectives
6. Logistics

PLAN CAREFULLY AND THOROUGHLY FOR THE SESSION
Plan out the timing of the session, but be flexible. Working with large groups of 20 to 60 people takes longer in each phase. Also, there is a greater chance someone will "bog" you down. You will need to allow "flex" time so you can adapt to individual paces, styles, questions, etc.

Design for the diversity of the group. One of the values of a large group is that you will be able to work off of the richness of different perspectives. However, remember that they will also enter the session with varying degrees of background about the topic. So design background information with that in mind.

Part of the planning for working with large groups must focus upon group management: sub-dividing the groups. When and for how long do you want to divide the large group? Who should be in the sub-groups? Who makes the decision as to who is in the small groups? Address this concern carefully as you plan the session.

Give careful consideration to numerous logistical details:
- Lighting
- Noise
- Doorways
- Temperature controls
- Room layout
- Table sizes
- Break food
- Signs for break out groups
- Complete the set up hours before session starts

GROUP MANAGEMENT
At the McNellis Company we best achieve success with large groups by table topping or by sub-dividing. The first approach to sub-dividing is to either have several facilitators, each assigned to lead a group, or a sub-group of the large group. A second approach is to table top. Table topping is simply working with the entire group simultaneously at their table groupings. Both techniques have clear advantages and disadvantages.

HINTS TO APPLY TO EITHER SUB-DIVIDING OR TABLE TOPPING
1. If you can influence or control the seating, or sub-group assignments, configure groupings so there is a diversity of perspectives at each table.
2. Be sure all tables have the necessary supplies. For table topping you will need the following at each table:
   - 50 or so yellow subbers (3"x5")
   - 10 or so yellow subbers (5"x8") for "upscaling"
   - 2 markers
   - a couple of killer balls
   - a sheet of dots

3. For sub-groups you will need a complete set of supplies. (See section 19)

TIPS ON SUB-GROUPING
1. This is the preferred method in managing a large group as you can maximize input and participation.
2. Ideal sub-groups would be 8 to 10 people. It also saves time. This is often not possible so try for no more than 10 to 15 in a group.
3. Set up each work area with boards, easels, and other supplies.
4. Plan out timing with the other facilitators. Plan out just as you would any session, but be sure to coordinate it so all of you are working cooperatively and on the same timeline. Agree which headers you will be working in the group.
5. Determine with the other facilitators whether you will complete the Concept in the sub-groups or in the large total group. It is easier to have each sub-group develop its own Concept. It is essential that every sub-group report to the total large group on their key ideas. The large groups can then dot down after each sub-group reports out on its top ideas.
6. If you have multiple groups working in the same large ball room, it is better to have three or more groups in the same large area than it is to have only two. With two groups, each group will tend to hear or focus (to some degree) on the voices from the other group. However, with three or more groups in the same area, it becomes difficult to concentrate on the auditory output of other groups.

TIPS FOR TABLE TOPPING
1. When availability of space, time or skilled facilitators prevent us from sub-dividing large groups, we can table top. The advantage is that all participants encounter the same experience. Time will really fly in working table tops because time gets broken into several small segments. However, manage your time carefully.

2. If you do not have tables, work them in small groups by turning chairs into circles. They can print on their laps. (Yes, they are the original "laptops"!)

3. Set up the room so the facilitator can freely work the crowd. Leave walking space between tables to go out and work the floor.

4. Generally it is good to work the first header with the entire group (maybe even the first two). This allows the facilitator to model listening, spinning, printing, etc.

5. Then move from the large group into working at their table in groups of 5 to 10 at the table. You can speed up things by having different tables look at different headers, or have different tables work on sub-sets of the same header.

© McNellis & Associates • Compression Planning Institute • 724-847-2120 • www.compressionplanning.com

6. When table topping, ask the group to work in the explorative phase for a set number of minutes. Have them use small yellow cards in the explorative. Then give them a few minutes to focus and reprint onto large yellow cards. Then ask each group to report on their top ideas. Be possessive of your time. Limit them on time, it keeps them focused and creative.

7. Depending upon the number of participants in a large group, all cards which are pinned up on boards may need to be upscaled. When you upscale, your printer must fill out the whole card so people can clearly see it. Make the printing large!

8. Example:
   a. Explore/create at least 8 ideas in the next 6 minutes.
   b. Focus (probably by discussion) on the top 2 during the next 2 minutes.
   c. Reprint - one minute.
   d. Report out from each table. Caution - watch out for speech making and "time eaters." Monitor and structure reports. Each table needs only 30 seconds to report.

9. The steps in #8 above can be repeated several times if you like. How much you table top and how much you work as a large group is a judgment call. The issue is how to get the most out of your time and the participants'.

10. After your explorative phase, determine how many dots are needed per participant - an advantage of the 5"x8" subber is that it provides ample room to dot.

11. Move into your Concept with a large group just as you would with a small group.

12. In working a large group using large table tops, be sure you collect all the smaller yellow cards under the appropriate header. Recruit someone in the group to do that for you so it occurs when a group reports out.

13. The disadvantage of working large groups with upscale cards is you quickly devour board space. You can get 6 rows of 5"x8" cards across a board and 8 cards down. That means about 48 ideas per board, when upscaling.

14. If you have a large number of participants, for example 60, two tips on dotting:
    - First you can put blank 3"x5" (or any color and size) cards along side each idea so there are places to dot.
    - Second, you can ask 2 people, as representatives, from each group/table to come up and dot for the table.

PLAN TO COMPLETE ORGANIZATION AND COMMUNICATION IN SMALL GROUP
In working with larger groups, it may well be appropriate to state up front that the purpose is to generate ideas/input. A NON-PURPOSE: to complete the plan.

However, if you do complete the final phases of the Master Model, it is often more effective to do that in smaller groups with carefully selected participants. Completion of the Organization phase and the Communication can often be very sensitive, as well as laborious for a large group.

Spinning/Churning

Spinning is the art of developing raw thoughts into rich ideas which can be acted upon. It is going from vagueness to specificity.

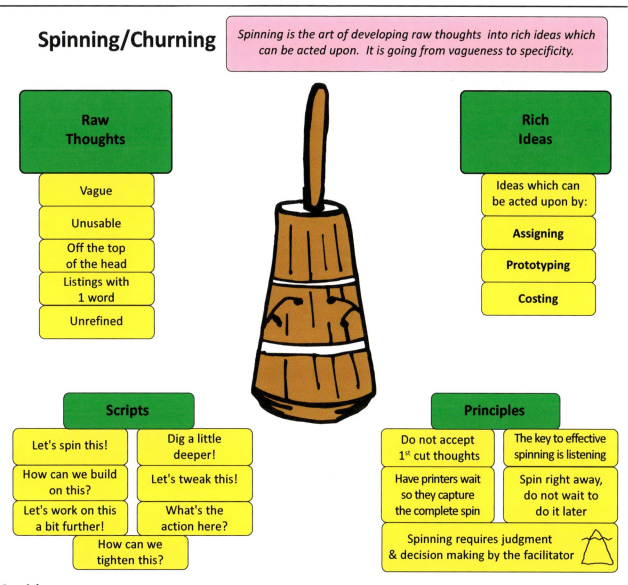

Raw Thoughts
- Vague
- Unusable
- Off the top of the head
- Listings with 1 word
- Unrefined

Rich Ideas
- Ideas which can be acted upon by:
- Assigning
- Prototyping
- Costing

Scripts
- Let's spin this!
- Dig a little deeper!
- How can we build on this?
- Let's tweak this!
- Let's work on this a bit further!
- What's the action here?
- How can we tighten this?

Principles
- Do not accept 1st cut thoughts
- The key to effective spinning is listening
- Have printers wait so they capture the complete spin
- Spin right away, do not wait to do it later
- Spinning requires judgment & decision making by the facilitator

Special notes

Sometimes a crazy or off-the-wall idea can actually be a high potential idea. You need to drive for the richness behind it. Rather than rejecting it as silly, ask "What is the principle behind what you just said?" Pull out several key principles and facilitate around the principles.

When confronted with a group member who is highly negative (one who is an expert at killer phrases) spin off the negativeness with a question like, "What can we do to make it work? How can we get it into the budget? What are some ways to get management to buy it? etc." Simply take the killer phrase and turn it around by facilitating the group to make it workable.

Spinning is not simply developing a new header and listing under it.

Examples of Spinning from Raw Thoughts to Rich Ideas

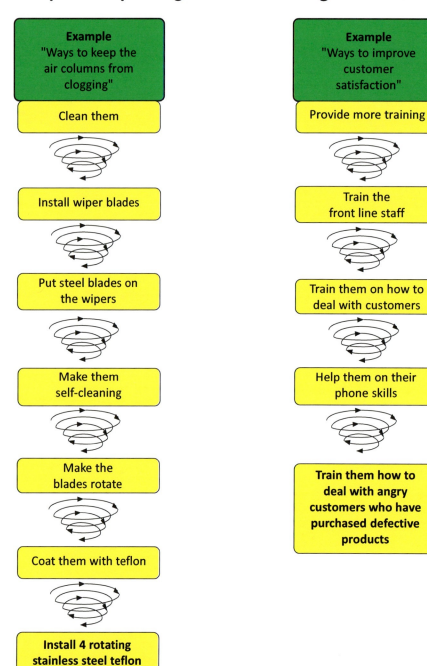

Supplemental reading - Facilitating an off-site Retreat

Congratulations if you are leading an off-site retreat! In my experience, over the past 25 years of leading off-site, strategic retreats, I know you will be in for something extra special. Off-site retreats are some of the most challenging, fascinating, and rewarding work that can be done with the Compression Planning process. Logistically, they are more of a challenge because you are working with a site where you frequently do not have control over the elements. Let me share with you 25+ years of experience in pulling one of these off from a logistics standpoint. I hope I can provide some useful hints and save you many headaches.

When we are contracted with to do an off-site retreat, we immediately start to work with our client in finding an off-site location. If possible, we visit the location and tightly eyeball it as well as experience the site. We have worked in the best of sites, and well, having worked early on in some of the "not-so-best" of sites, the importance of getting to know your surroundings became quite evident. So, my advice to you…if at all possible visit the site before you plan the retreat. Last year I was on 4 airplanes in one day to visit a location because I was uncomfortable with the room layouts that were faxed to me. It is a good thing I saw the location as well as spent time with the staff. It was a unique arrangement where the rooms had to be set up and taken down several times in one day and without full cooperation of the staff we never would have pulled it off.

When at the site, the first thing I always do is sit in the chairs. It sounds a little elementary, but chairs make or break a session. You want your participants to be comfortable and not distracted by a second-rate, uncomfortable, banquet chair they will be in for a day or two or more. I find that chairs without arms, but with cushions, wheels and the possibility of adjusting the height are best. Big, bulky, boardroom chairs are a disaster.

The second thing I look for is lighting. Lighting is vital to the success of your retreat. The absolute ideal is to have as much natural light as possible. Be aware of where the sun comes up and goes down. Get the east/west orientation and see if the windows (high and low) will or can be protected during the time the sunlight will be hitting the windows. Rooms with fluorescent lighting without windows will be a challenge - avoid them at all costs. Many country clubs have horrible lighting in rooms that are primarily for cocktails and dinners. Insufficient lighting is simply an energy drain.

A strategic retreat is one where key people are frequently addressing make-or-break issues and paying attention to these details only makes sense. Once I read that the Boston Celtic star Larry Bird would get to the Boston Gardens before a game and crawl all over it checking every inch of the floor. Then he would dive on the floor in many places all over the court. He had similar routines for other arenas he played in. That's a pro. That's being prepared. I think a strategic retreat is vastly more important than a basketball game and we should treat the physical environment as such.

The next thing I do is sit at all sides of the table. Where are the legs? Will people bang their knees on the legs? It is critical that the corners of the table match up when put next to each other. Why hotels and conference centers even buy tables with differing heights baffles me. The best tables I've come across are lightweight, 30-36 inches-wide, between six and eight feet long, and the legs are positioned so there is no way you will hit your knees. We sit at the tables and attempt everything possible to bang our knees. Strategic retreats often lend themselves to moving tables around and restructuring the environment so pay close attention to the tables.

Big boardroom tables with massive stuffy chairs may look impressive but are not good for Compression Planning.

You also need to develop a strong relationship with the staff. How often do they hold business retreats? What is their specialty? You want someone who is adept at dealing with businesses and their special needs. You do not want a place that specializes in weddings, birthday parties and Bar mitzvahs. Also, get to know the intricacies of their shipping department. If you are shipping materials, such as your storyboards, find out what all needs to go on the label. Often times we include the sales person, our name, the name of the retreat, and the dates. Many centers want you to arrange for your supplies to arrive the day before the retreat begins and pick them up the day it ends or the following morning. I always try to get the supplies there at least two days early...just in case!

This is may sound elementary, but have the staff set up a water station instead of putting water and glasses on the work tables. This frees up the space and eliminates the chance of spilling accidents.

The food you choose is also very important. Go healthy! Choose fruits, and whole grain bagels, and muffins for AM instead of sugary donuts, and vegetables, cheeses, crackers, and nuts in PM, instead of sugary items like cookies. Go light on lunch - filling and tasty, but light. Avoid heavy foods and turkey.

You will also want to pay attention to sound - not only between rooms, but also outside in the hallways, outside of the building (i.e. next to a swimming pool), and pay special attention to service corridors as well. A good conference site will not have noisy corridors!

And last, but not least...schedule a break every 90 minutes. Encourage people to step outside, get a breath of fresh air and make sure you set a timer so they know when the break is over. We give people a 13-minute break.

Oh yeah, one last thing...have the "top person" address how you will handle cell phone interruptions. If the number one person makes the commitment to turn off their cell phone in front of the group, you will have everyone else follow suit. Arrange for the staff to post messages on a board and advise the participants to look for them on breaks.

Natural groups

When designing a retreat there is normally a natural group that should be included. This group includes any, or many, of the following: board of directors, executive team, owners plus key direct reports, senior staff, project team, staff group, a functional group like marketing, cross functional multi layer project teams, key company players plus vendors or customers or both, management and labor leaders. The list goes on.

I am frequently asked "What is the ideal sized group?" My answer is 1 person. Adding more people complicates it.

Seriously though, I think you want to have the smallest number of people that can accomplish the purpose of your retreat. I've led them for 2-3 people and for 25 or more because of the purpose of the retreat. The important thing is to ask serious questions on the front end about the purpose and expected outcomes of the retreat.

When I hear someone wants to lead a retreat of 40 or 50 people and do it alone, I shake my head. As professionals we facilitate groups that size with a minimum of three professional facilitators and frequently logistical support people. If you face facilitating a large group, call because we have special material we can send you to give you ideas.

It is important to look at the group to make sure it isn't too insular. Having everyone from one level, in one function, frequently turns into a "pity party." Having a broader viewpoint or set of perspectives helps keep the group from being excessively insular.

"Unnatural groups"- Special people to invite to an offsite

As a general principle the deeper and wider in an organization you go the richer the output of the retreat. So, depending on the organization, the purpose of the retreat and the size of the organization and the sensitivity of the issues, some of the following considerations could be part of your criteria for inviting people:

1. Whose nose will be bent out of joint and who will be long term destructive if they aren't part of the initial effort? Sorry to say this happens but it is real world. I'd rather have them there and be part of things than have to fight them downstream in a process.

2. Who brings a unique perspective like a key customer or joint venture partner? Who is a non-competing leader in the same field that faced similar situations and would be available and willing to help?

3. Include your banker, lawyer, CPA, architect, marketing firm and other special talents that are outside your group.

4. Past leaders of the organization or function are frequently incredibly rich contributors.

5. Having a corporate leader included in a divisional offsite - not as a presenter, but as a contributor and participant pays off with increased insights and strengthening of relationships.

I am giving you general principles to consider. You know the people, personalities and politics, but hopefully these ideas stimulate an idea or two.

I am 100% against having "observers" in a retreat. Everyone is a participant, no matter what. That is why we have the participants do the roles of the storyboarding, like printing and pinning. In the thousands of sessions I've done I can only think of four where we had someone other than participants
do the printing.

When the top person (CEO, etc) suggests that maybe they should not be there (because they have such strong personalities and they don't want to stifle the discussion) my response is: be there. I'll show them the best place to sit so they are not in the "power position" and as out of direct line of sight as possible. You want the ideas bouncing off the storyboard and not filtering through the client or top person. As a facilitator, you need to address the role of the top person. Enlightened leaders are extremely aware of their role and want to play it carefully. They typically want to listen to their people a great deal. You may want to negotiate a set of signals with them if you think they are over participating.

Special Situations to stimulate your thinking when designing retreats
The following are some situations I've facilitated over the years. I am not mentioning companies/ organizations to protect their privacy.

Situation #1
A company, their distribution managers and 15 or so of their top customers set out to figure out how to sell more together. At first the customer was quite aloof. Once we were into the session for about 30 minutes his attitude changed about 200 %. He was wondering why the company wasn't doing a certain thing and the company was wondering why he wasn't supporting them - $5 million was dedicated right then for a mutual move and both sides were ecstatic. We put several teams together consisting of a key customer, 6 distributors, sales people and marketing staff. There were 15 such teams. At the end of the session I facilitated, the once aloof customer wanted to buy drinks

for everyone. He wanted a group photo and must have shaken everyone's hand about 10 times!

Situation #2
The top 8 executives of a company and their spouses asked me to facilitate them on mutual issues. It was something. The spouses (mostly female) asked me to facilitate them separately and help them address some incredibly tough issues. Then their partners were summoned and they received a storyboard presentation of the spouses concerns and solutions. Most were adopted on the spot. In light of the Enron situation one that pops to mind was the spouses said their lives were tied to the company and they wanted in-depth quarterly financial presentations on the state of the business and that happened. Another I remember was setting up a system where spouses helped others when a move was made where the exec moved off quickly and was all excited in the new job. The spouse remaining had to frequently prepare and sell the house, organize the move deal with the kids, and handle a change of career for themselves with little assistance.

The energy and passion of their spouses and the subjects they surfaced dumbfounded the execs and the solutions they almost demanded. It was fun to facilitate that portion of their retreat.

Situation #3
Another one that will always stand out was with a management team of a company owned by one person. I suggested his wife participate for the entire three days. She hired a sitter for their kids and was a 100% participant . They made two absolutely crucial decisions one of which increased their profits by 50% in one year. What was so memorable was at the end, when we did the YAMA (where we give everyone a chance to share their closing thoughts) she said she had three things to say:

1. Without being part of the decision making process on the major move, which proved to be so successful, she didn't think she could have appreciated it.
2. She had never truly seen the managers of the company in a real situation that wasn't mostly social and she came to appreciate how bright, dedicated and determined they were.
3. She frequently lived in fear that if something happened to her husband, and he couldn't run the organization, she now had the confidence that the company could continue without him. She told the group, to her husband's amazement, that she would probably sleep peacefully for the first time in years. It was a poignant moment.

Situation #4
Many times I've led groups where someone was on their first day with the organization. Several have included people who have been hired and haven't started working yet. It accelerates that new person into the organization like crazy.

Recruiting People and Preparing them for an Offsite Retreat
Do it personally. Don't do it by memo. Don't send an e-mail or letter except to confirm the details. Make it special. Tell them how important it is that they participate. Tell them how it will be different and you need them to participate.

Preparation Materials for a Retreat

Be extremely careful about what you provide the participants in advance for preparation. Here are my Top 5 Retreat Sins:

1. Sending everyone a book by the latest guru with the expectation people will read it. Some read it, some skim it and most don't remember it and fake it. If you must send something, send a comprehensive summary and highlight the few key parts. Be extremely selective.

2. Having state of the organization speeches by key leaders with Power Point presentations. Again, be extremely selective. When top leaders ask me what they should say in their opening, I suggest they say anything they want to as long as they do it in three minutes or LESS. There is normally a presidential moment where the top person has significant things to share, but frequently they can be inserted more casually along the way.

3. Golf. People should golf on their own time. And many people don't golf.

4. Competitive sports like softball, racquetball even volleyball tournaments. It seems like the pressure of retreats, especially strategic ones, is such that the energies and passions get really heated up. Many times I've seen competitive sporting events send one or more people to an emergency ward.

5. Booze. Thank goodness U.S. Business, in my experience, has moved away from the mandatory cocktail parties. I encourage our clients to minimize or eliminate this type of activity.

The last 2 webcasts were focused on preparation for an offsite retreat including the logistics of working with a site as well as determining who should attend. This issue focuses on key design areas you should address for an offsite session.

For me the absolute key item for success is the relationship you have with the client (if you are not the client).

The best retreats I've facilitated have been where..

1. The clients were clear in their expectations. They weren't having an offsite because "we did it last year" or some other general reason. There was a specific purpose as well as a clearly articulated expected outcome.

2. They were deeply engaged in the design of the retreat. That doesn't mean they did all the detailed design work, but that they were intimately involved and had 100% buy-in to the process being used.

3. They made themselves available. It takes a lot of work to finalize a design to make sure the time being spent ensures a "positive ROI" on the participants time. They'll say things like "call me anytime you need anything." "Call me at home if you have questions." It's a great client who makes himself or herself available because they respect and understand the process.

4. If too much of the work is delegated to support staff, then you better watch out. The time and expense of an offsite is too valuable for the key leader and his/her close associates not to be intimately involved in the design.

Last week at a business development conference, I heard the point that one hour of planning will save FOUR hours of execution time. I think a corollary of that is every hour of planning for an offsite retreat will increase the quality of your sessions by four or by ten or even more.

© McNellis & Associates • Compression Planning Institute • 724-847-2120 • www.compressionplanning.com

The key is the focus on and clarity of the purposes. I am not telling you anything new, just reiterating that it is especially crucial to have clarity for your offsite. The time allotment really can be interrupted if there aren't clear, specific, measurable and verifiable purposes.

For a great example of someone who forced senior leaders to get clarity, see Power User Interview with Joe Fonte of Delphi. Joe was able to facilitate an offsite where they realized a savings of $1.5M per year in a little over a day using Compression Planning. The retreat was successful because of Joe's diligence in getting the top people to nail down the specific purposes of the sessions.

A few key questions I find helpful when designing something as critical as an offsite planning session are...

- What is special or distinct about this time that prompts you to do this session now? Normally something critical is driving the situation and it is important to understand that need.

- Are you intending to use a general planning approach or do you need a custom designed one? A general one is the SWOT (strengths, weaknesses, opportunities, threats) along with Mission/Vision etc. A more specific, custom designed one is around a few key questions. I find people are tired of the traditional template driven planning sessions and want something custom designed.

I'd appreciate any of your thoughts and insights. Every design alert I've done for someone designing an offsite retreat called for custom design versus general templates. E-mail me at jerry@mcnellisco.com with any observations!

- Instead of the Mission and Vision driven sessions, consider going for unique positioning sessions. Headers like :

What will we be absolutely untouchable in?
What areas won't we be involved with?
What will we do that absolutely no one else will do for their clients?

You will find a refreshing type of energy driving the generation of ideas when using these types of questions. You will get highly practical and tactical ideas instead of "save the planet types of statements" and ideas that are so general and vague that they are hard to drive for true action.

A question that always comes up, and I mentioned it before and want to address it again, is "What do I send people for background?" Be extremely careful about preparing people ahead of time for the retreat. My caution to you is - Do not send the latest book by the guru of your field and expect people to read it prior to the retreat. They won't. Or at least don't expect all to read it. A few might. Most won't. A few will scan the book and fake it. If they've spent their lives in the industry, any last minute cramming probably isn't going to do a lot to enhance their knowledge.

Rather I suggest you build the content into the session background (graphically is best) and sprinkle it throughout the sessions.

At the end of Exploration

1. Review purposes of the session
2. Confer with the client - "Have we delivered the purpose for you?"
3. Decide if dotting would be useful and if not, go straight to a break
4. Determine the number and colors of dots you will want to give each participant
5. Sometimes it is helpful to put the number of dots on a header that you want participants to use on the subbers under that header
6. Tell participants the length of the break
7. Give instructions to dot during and immediately after the break

During the Break

1. Confer with the client on concept headers - "How would it be most helpful to sort, select and organize this material for you?"
2. Propose concept headers that you created prior to the session
3. Pin up focus guidelines
4. Set up storyboard with concept headers
5. Put up a retrieval envelope

During Focus Phase

1. Review guidelines
2. Explain retrieval envelope
3. Explain the concept headers
4. Move the cards - make preliminary decisions - sort the ideas down to the manageable few

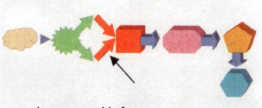

During the Concept Phase

1. Merge ideas/restate ideas
2. Make commitments
3. Try to eliminate as much as you can
4. Aim for the key ideas you intend to do so well that people have to come to you to get what it is that you have - strive for uniqueness

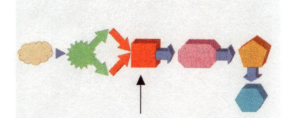

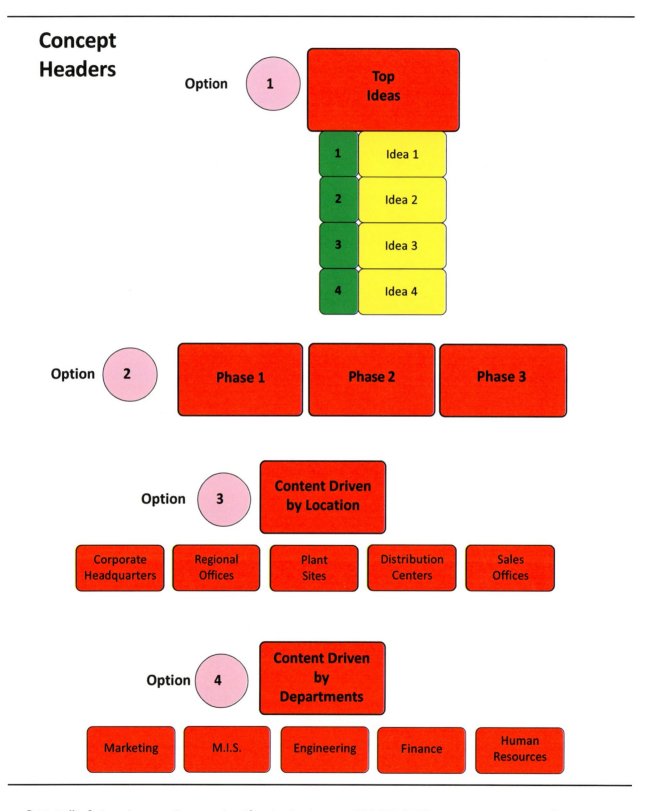

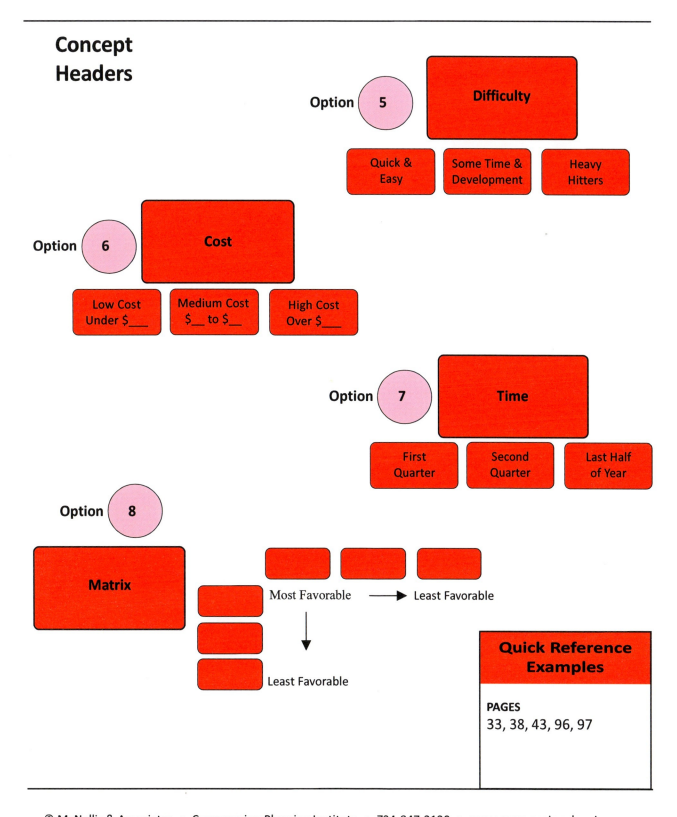

Supplemental notes for focusing into Concept

At the end of exploration, do a final check with the client to review the **Purpose of this Session** and decide if the basis has been laid to now focus it down to achieve the purpose as stated or revised.

If the purpose statement has held, prior to the session, you should be able to anticipate how you will do the categories under the headers that the group will work and what your concept headers (the pink cards) will say. Or if you have not pre-thought this aspect, which we strongly suggest you project this out in advance, it should become clear at this point.

If you and the client seem to be clear on how to proceed with the dotting, have the pinner take down the green explore guideline cards used during the exploration. Review the red focus cards with the group and have the pinner put them on the board. If it is not clear to you and the client as to how the dotting is going to work, send the group on a break and decide with the client how to proceed and then review with the group the red cards and dotting procedure when they return.

In general, if you are doing an idea session or your purpose states that you want, for example, "the top 5 ideas," you will dot to bubble up the immediate keepers to fulfill the purpose.

In general, if you are doing a planning session or your purpose states, for example "to determine all the components of the plan," you will dot to eliminate.

There may be times when a header is a data dump and neither dotting to bubble up nor dotting to eliminate makes sense or is needed.

If you have a large group, you may wish to divide them in two, asking one half to dot for the first six minutes and then break and the other half to do the reverse.

If dotting to bubble up, look at the purpose(s) and determine if you need to keep dotting segregated by headers to get representation from the various headers or if the dotting is to be done overall. It all depends on how the client has stated the purpose. In general, give one dot for every 7-10 cards to be dotted in a category. It is not related to the number stated in the purpose, i.e. if the purpose states "to generate 5 ideas," it does not mean you give five dots unless the number of cards to be dotted just happens to be between 35-50. You can code either the headers or purpose with the number of dots you want them to use, just to serve as a visual reminder. Also, ask the client if there are any last reminders to the participants so they will spend their dots in the most meaningful manner. If desired, you can have different departments dot in different colors if it is beneficial. Ask participants to dot only one dot per card and try to not be influenced as to where others have placed their dots. Talk with the client to see if they want to dot in a different color and have them dot last so as not to unintentionally influence the dotting of others. If you are doing a double master model, you will explore twice and dot to focus into concept twice. Basically, you will use the results of the first dotting as the basis to go out and explore the second time and then dot the second exploration.

If you are going to dot to eliminate, explain to the participants that they do not have to dot any cards if they feel all of them "fit" or are irrelevant under a certain header. Conversely, if they feel certain cards don't belong, they can dot as many cards as they deem appropriate but after the dotting, they will be asked to explain their thinking to the group. If a card has a dot on it, after brief discussion, the options are the 4Rs: remove dot, remove card, reword, or review later as indicated with a note on a small green card next to it.

Concept - *Supplemental notes*

After dotting, bring the cards with the most dots over to the pink headers you have created. This may be as simple as "Top Ideas for..." as cued off the words in the purpose. In a planning session, the cards that remain after dotting to eliminate, then probably fulfill your purpose statement and the pink card may actually remain the same as "Components of the plan." For ease, you can just leave them in their current placement on the board.

You can either merge before or after dotting with the preference being after dotting for reasons discussed during the training. With the caution not to over merge and if anyone does not see it as a merger, they will remain separate. Ask the group to check, in the following order, for the four aspects of merging. Using the example of "Top 5 Ideas" - do any of the five merge together? Do any that did not come over merge into the top five that came over? Are there related cards that did not come over that if we had merged before dotting would have had sufficient strength to come over? And finally, the last call of does anyone feel very strongly about a card that did not come over and they want to review it with the group? None of the cards will go away and the client can reflect on them later but we need to help the client get it down to a manageable few as indicated in the purpose statement.

Remember that during this phase, it is ok to judge, analyze and have some discussion, but it should be focused discussion, not a two hour meeting!

Unless the client feels that a second cut, as outlined on pages 10-2 and 10-3 would be helpful, you are finished with the focus and concept phase. These two phases are intertwined and another way of stating these phases is "what are your immediate keepers to fulfill the purpose and what is a logical way to organize and label these immediate keepers." If your purpose is very clear and the headers match the purpose and consequently help achieve the purpose, the road map for this portion will be clear.

© McNellis & Associates • Compression Planning Institute • 724-847-2120 • www.compressionplanning.com

Compression Planning Decision Assist Grid

Proposal	Contribution to Purpose	Costs (out-of-pocket) Start-up _____ On-going _____	Time (payroll) Start-up _____ On-going _____	Major Impacts on the Organization (+ & -)	Difficulty (implementation) Start-up _____ On-going _____	Major Side Effects (+ & -) Primary, Secondary, Tertiary
Proposed Decision						
Proposed Policy						
Proposed Action						
Proposed _____						

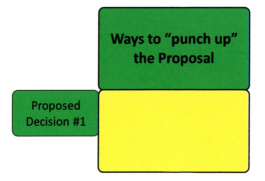

Action Plan - Instructions

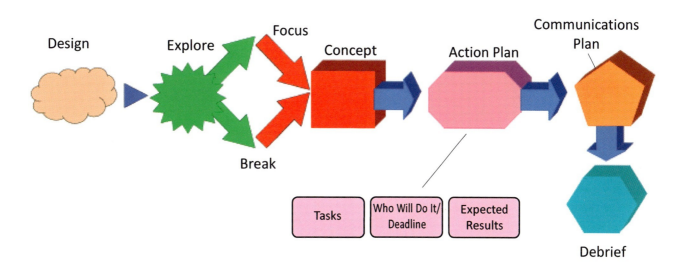

Instructions

1. Determine if you want to task at the micro or macro level
2. Identify the critical few next steps to move this issue/project to the next level
3. List all of the tasks first
4. Go across and nail down who will complete the task and by when
5. Often it is helpful to change or interpret the second header as "Who will oversee the task," "Who will be responsible," "Who will lead the effort"
6. Expected Results - by completing the task, what specifically is the deliverable?

Quick Reference Examples
PAGES   34, 39, 44, 98a, 98b, 98c, 98d, 99

© McNellis & Associates • Compression Planning Institute • 724-847-2120 • www.compressionplanning.com

Action Plan - *Options*

Action Plan Option #1

Low Hanging Fruit

1 — Have Brian conduct our meetings or other designated person ●● ●● | Name / Deadline

Have clear objective identified for every meeting - not just information but ●● actionable ●

Revisit our weekly meetings so one is a "work mtg." and the next is informational ● ● ●

2 — Leverage budget ● formulation Account managers ● ● ● | Name / Deadline

3 — Suggest to vendor ● that a director/ ● specialist would be helpful and is needed | Name / Deadline

Some Time, Cost, Effort

4 — Get TD feedback at regular meeting with agenda of PAE ● projects that ● ● need input ●● | Name / Deadline

Engage the TD program managers ●●● ●● ●

Explore getting TD input into the development of our strategic plan ● ● ●

5 — Develop a database ● of spokes available and define criteria ● for choosing spokes ● ● ● ● | Name / Deadline

Standardize" the spoke selection projects ● ● ●

6 — ● Develop a master ● calendar of who is working on what & when (non-contract ● stuff) ● | Name / Deadline

With well "spun"/developed ideas, you can quickly assign a name and a deadline and post it next to the Idea.

Post the Name/Deadline card next to the top idea which is often a "summary" of the merged cards.

Put the name of the person who will lead the effort to see that it gets done.

This method works well with dedicated project teams that meet on a "regular" basis.

© McNellis & Associates • Compression Planning Institute • 724-847-2120 • www.compressionplanning.com

Action Plan Option #2

	Low Hanging Fruit		Tasks	Who will do it / Deadline	Expected Results
1	Have Brian conduct our meetings or other designated person ●● ●●	1	Identify which meetings it makes sense for Brian to lead	Neil / Nov. 12	A master calendar of dates and teams highlighting meetings Brian will lead
	Have clear objective identified for every meeting - not just information but ●● actionable ●		Get Brian registered for the next Compression Planning Workshop in Pgh.	Brian / Nov. 5	Brian attends excellent CP workshop and is highly skilled at leading meetings
	Revisit our weekly meetings so one is a "work mtg." and the next is informational ● ● ●		Determine what supplies Brain will need to lead the designated meetings	Shelly / Nov. 10	Fully equipped meeting room with all necessary supplies
2	Leverage budget ● formulation Account managers ● ● ●	2	Contact John in accounting to get his recommendation	Wayne / Oct. 30	A detailed plan on how to implement by end of year
3	Suggest to vendor ● that a director/ ●● specialist would be helpful and is needed		Ask Stephanie to give a presentation at the next Acct. Mgrs. meeting	Wayne / Oct. 30	Have all acct. mgrs. on board and fully understanding at next meeting
		3	Contact top 3 vendors and get their input and explain why	Lauren / Nov. 7	2 committed specialists that will give us 1 hour of input per month

1. Assign each Top Idea a number.
2. Identify 2-3 key next steps per idea - macro, not micro.
3. If team developing the action plan is also the implementation team, consider sub-dividing per top idea and have team member come back with tasks.
4. Number each set of tasks to correspond to the top idea as a reference - all ideas under Action Plan #1 correspond to the #1 idea under Top Ideas.

© McNellis & Associates • Compression Planning Institute • 724-847-2120 • www.compressionplanning.com

Action Plan Option #3

Low Hanging Fruit	Tasks	Who will do it / Deadline	Expected Results
1 — Have Brian conduct our meetings or other designated person •• ••	Identify a team/committee who will take ownership of each top idea	Neil / Nov. 12	A dedicated, available team to do the necessary research and work
Have clear objective identified for every meeting - not just information but actionable •• •	Run each top idea through the Decision Assist Filter Grid for further development	Brian / Nov. 5	An understanding of the impact, costs and feasibility of each idea
Revisit our weekly meetings so one is a "work mtg." and the next is informational • • •	Develop plan to present to senior management for their approval	Shelly / Nov. 10	A go/no-go decision on each of the top ideas from senior management
2 — Leverage budget formulation Account managers • • • •	Develop an implementation calendar for the entire project	Wayne / Oct. 30	A workflow master calendar with milestones, deadlines & goals
3 — Suggest to vendor that a director/specialist would be helpful and is needed •• ••			

Look at the Top Ideas as ONE idea versus individual ideas.

1. Identify key next steps to implementation of the entire plan.
   This is Macro-Master Planning.

This sets expectations and gets the "ball rolling" knowing that a lot more work needs to be done. The work is often times turned over to a team or committee for further refinement.

It is still important to identify the WHO and DEADLINE to establish accountability and show that work is going to be done.

© McNellis & Associates • Compression Planning Institute • 724-847-2120 • www.compressionplanning.com

Action Plan Option #4

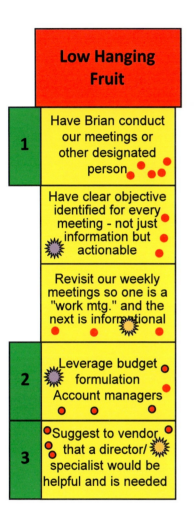

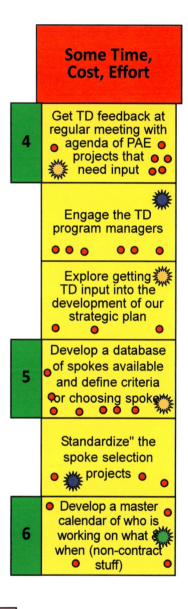

With well "spun"/developed ideas, you can quickly assign a name by having individuals dot the ideas they are willing to complete.

Assign each person a different colored dot or sticker and develop a reference card like the blue card in the middle with names and corresponding dots.

It's helpful to keep the reference card if the team meets frequently and does not change.

Action Plan - *Micro Planning*

Final Action Idea

A = 1 or more person(s) as well as rest of team

Elements of Action Idea	Tasks	Who Will Lead The Task	Deadline	Methods of Measuring Progress/Results	Methods for Reporting Progress to <u>A</u>
Description of Element #1	Action Statement #1	Person responsible for task #1	Specific deadline for task #1	For Task #1	For Task #1
Description of Element #2	Action Statement #2	Person responsible for task #2	Specific deadline for task #2	For Task #2	For Task #2
Description of Element #3	Action Statement #3	Person responsible for task #3	Specific deadline for task #3	For Task #3	For Task #3
Description of Element #4	Action Statement #4	Person responsible for task #4	Specific deadline for task #4	For Task #4	For Task #4
Description of Element #5	Action Statement #5	Person responsible for task #5	Specific deadline for task #5	For Task #5	For Task #5
Description of Element #6	Action Statement #6	Person responsible for task #6	Specific deadline for task #6	For Task #6	For Task #6
Description of Element #7	Action Statement #7	Person responsible for task #7	Specific deadline for task #7	For Task #7	For Task #7
Description of Element #8	Action Statement #8	Person responsible for task #8	Specific deadline for task #8	For Task #8	For Task #8

© McNellis & Associates • Compression Planning Institute • 724-847-2120 • www.compressionplanning.com

Action Plan - *FAQ*

Question:
We seem to drift off when we come to the action plan. Any comments on how we can focus more on tasks?

Answer:
You are not alone! Sometimes there is a natural let-down when you come to the Action and Communication Plans. You've done some heavy idea generation and moved into concept and no doubt, you're a bit tired.

One thing you can do is take an extended break, maybe even come back the next day when energy levels are back up. But, let's assume you are going straight through to the finish.

First, decide if you are going to plan at a macro or micro level. Sometimes you don't know enough yet to get down to nitty-gritty planning. You may need more information, possibly another session. Those can become tasks.

A lot of times tasking may involve assigning a person or persons to do next steps you have identified, and in those cases, they will do an action plan around that task when they begin work.

Basically, ask yourselves "what do we need to do now to move this project to either the next step or to completion?"

All those things you need to do become tasks, then you assign responsibility and deadlines. Don't shortcut.

Once you've done that, move on to Communication and Debrief. You'll find your projects move more quickly, more completely and more smoothly when you devote serious time and energy to each step of the Master Planning Model.

Time saving Action Planning Tips and Tricks

1. Subdivide the group. Assign one or two people to take on each individual idea. Have them propose who should be responsible for overseeing that part of the plan (not necessarily the person who will do the task.)

   Give each team 4-6 minutes to generate the tasks, proposed who will do it and proposed deadlines. Report back to the entire group and rework if necessary.

2. Use dots for different people in a natural work team. If you meet weekly, there is no need to assign deadlines. All tasks need to be completed by the next time you meet. You can dot the concept cards - those ideas that are the deliverables of your purpose

   Keep one master card with the dots and names and you can use it for every session!

3. Use "greenies" and place a persons name in the left hand corner, draw a diagonal line, and then the deadline in the bottom right corner. Pin the card next to the concept/deliverable card.

© McNellis & Associates • Compression Planning Institute • 724-847-2120 • www.compressionplanning.com

Communication Plan - *Instructions*

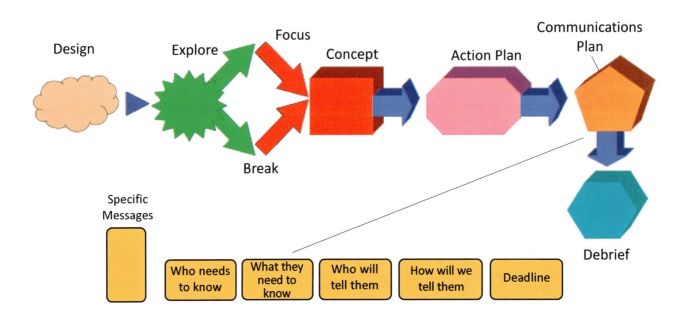

Hints

1. Under the header "Who needs to know," list on separate yellow cards anyone or groups of people impacted by the project, meeting or conference

2. Now go back to "Specific messages" and list each piece of information that anyone listed under "Who needs to know," would need to know. Put each detailed message on a separate yellow card. Give each "Specific message" a number by putting up sequentially numbered green cards beside the "Specific Message"

3. Go over to "What they need to know" and put separate yellow cards with the numbers of the Specific messages beside each person listed under "Who needs to know." Example of a yellow card: "2,5,7,9,12,14"

4. Under "How we will tell them," simply list on a yellow card a how that person will be communicated to

5. Identify who will convey the messages to each person or group of people in #1.

6. Determine deadlines

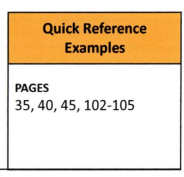

Quick Reference Examples
PAGES 35, 40, 45, 102-105

© McNellis & Associates • Compression Planning Institute • 724-847-2120 • www.compressionplanning.com

Communication Plan - *Wedding Example*

Specific Messages

Who are our clients?

1. Buy a birthday cake for Alisha and Grandpa for the rehearsal dinner
2. Ask the reception hall if they have any non-smoking signs
3. Time, place and directions to the rehearsal dinner and note that appropriate dress is casual
4. Set up time to get in the church on the day of the wedding is 9:00 a.m.
5. Set up time on Saturday at B&B Banquet Hall is between 9:00 – 1:00 a.m.
6. The arrival time at the church on Saturday is 1:00 p.m.
7. Provide a list of what pictures we want taken
8. Provide a list of people we want on the video at the ceremony and the reception
9. The total number of people attending the reception is 155
10. Pass out directions to the reception hall from the church
11. Bring white Christmas lights to the reception hall
12. Bring fresh ivy to surround the cake table
13. Get someone to arrange the flowers on the top of the cake
14. Arrange to pick up and store the Anniversary cake
15. The cake will be in a burgundy napkin wrap
16. Confirm the menu with B&B for food and drinks
17. Arrange gathering of all the cookies
18. Let people know when to bring the cookies
19. Have the DJ do all of the announcements at the reception
20. Announce the time the reception starts at the end of the wedding ceremony
21. Arrange to have mini-napkins for the cookie table
22. Buy mini paper plates for the cookie table
23. Provide B&B with a room set-up for the head table
24. Announce the start time for dinner
25. Do not use the cheesy paper bells at B&B
26. Have four reserved tables – 2 tens and 2 eights
27. Get cups for the reception hall bar
28. Have umbrellas available for the wedding party and guests in case it rains
29. Create a welcome basket for the women's restroom to include hand lotion, hair spray, etc.
30. Do not put out ash trays except for outside the reception hall
31. Ask Connie if she has a backdrop for the head table
32. Bring the pew bows to the reception hall
33. Decorate the tables with fish bowls and fish
34. Make hotel arrangements for out of town guests at the Holiday Inn
35. Check to see if there is enough white ribbon
36. Provide an information packet at hotel for guests – include local attractions from the chamber of commerce
37. Find a place to freeze the ice sculpture
38. Get bolts of white ribbon from Stephanie to put on the chairs
39. Bring silk flowers to decorate the arch at B&B
40. Arrange location and details on the signature picture
41. The selected music – get to the right people – the DJ and the pianist and all singers
42. Stacey and Denise will be singing "Grow Old" and "The Lord's Prayer"
43. Tell the pianist she needs to play prelude music and postlude music
44. Determine who to give what money to and who gives it
45. Time, date and place for the rehearsal is – August 2, 1996 – 6:00 p.m. church, 7:30 at Dockers Restaurant
46. Provide and outline for the church ceremony

© McNellis & Associates • Compression Planning Institute • 724-847-2120 • www.compressionplanning.com

Communication Plan - *Wedding Example*

47. Get pictures to video memories of Stephanie and Pat
48. Take a copy of the invitation to the ceremony
49. Have a list of the bridal party and parents
50. Determine how to handle requests for extra pictures
51. Determine when all monies are due
52. Arrange to have Donna and Kelly be the servers at Dockers
53. Determine the bar details including amounts needed to purchase
54. Find someone to watch the cat and fish while in Venezuela on honeymoon
55. Tell Mark there is no parking on the street on Monday nights – street cleaning
56. Arrange time to pick up the tuxedos
57. Arrange for someone to return all of the tuxedos on Monday
58. Determine the car details and who rides with whom
59. Find someone to be in charge of decorating the cars
60. Arrange flowers for the mothers
61. Confirm all previous details with all vendors
62. Pin flowers on the people who get them
63. Take candle holders to the florist
64. Put signs leading to wedding and reception for out-of-towners
65. Tell the florist we do not need fern but we do need baby's breath for the reception tables
66. Order one more boutonniere for Pastor Lee and flowers for Denise
67. Get flight information for honeymoon
68. Date Stephanie needs her dress is June 27th
69. Find someone to press the dress
70. Determine what time the pictures will be taken
71. Makeup and hair can be done at Lazarus on Saturday morning at 9:00 a.m.
72. Take mirrors to and from the church for the bridal party
73. Designate rooms for dressing – party and non-party
74. Get details of jewelry and stockings
75. Assure that attire fits properly – try on before
76. Provide suggestions for attire for reception
77. Determine how many girls will go to Lazarus on Saturday morning
78. Confirm the time for appointment on Saturday morning
79. Find out if they do nails at Lazarus
80. Bring the sparkely blush
81. Determine who to tip and how much
82. Pat will tip the bartender ahead of time and ask that a tip jar not be put out
83. Find out of Constantina will come alter to fix hair and makeup
84. Get together on Thursday night if possible
85. Prepare a toast
86. Make sure you eat diner on Friday and lunch on Saturday
87. Get readings to people who need them
88. Find someone to clean the Arc van
89. Determine people who need wireless microphones
90. Find someone to help transport gifts from the hall to home
91. Develop a program for the bridal dinner
92. Decorate and bring the bird cage for cards
93. Bring a cake knife, unity candle and aisle runner

94. Take the CD player to the church to assure function before Friday's rehearsal
95. Monitor card box throughout the night and lock up the cards
96. Will stay at Steph's on Friday night
97. Bring bubble decorations from Sally's to Steph's
98. Arrange for Stacey to practice with the pianist
99. Confirm rooms at the Holiday Inn
100. Provide suggestions for the next best accommodations in town
101. Pass out programs during the ceremony
102. Ask to be greeters at the church
103. Create table tents for songs with "love" at the reception
104. Pass out bells and bubbles at the church
105. Bring signature matte to rehearsal dinner

Who Needs To Know	What They Need To Know	Who Needs To Know	What They Need To Know
Stephanie -bride	2,3,4,5,6,7,8,9,14,16,17,18,20,23,24, 26,28,29,31,36,37,38,39,45,46,52, 60,63,65,66,68,69,70,71,73,74,75, 77,78,80,83,84,86,90,92,93,102	Rich Evans -reader	3,6,10,46
Pat -groom	3,4,5,6,7,8,9,14,16,19,20,22,23,24, 26,27,30,34,36,40,44,45,46,47,48, 49,51,49,51,53,54,55,56,58,64,67, 70,73,75,81,82,86,87,88,89,93,94, 97,99,100,102,103,105	Benji the bartender	5,9,20,24,37,82
Sally Ursta -mother of the bride	3,4,5,6,10,13,15,24,26,28, 34,45,49,60,70,71,75,86,92	Lisa McNellis -sister of the groom	62,72,95
Sue McNellis -mother of the groom	1,4,5,6,12,13,26,33,36,45,56, 57,60,70,71,73,84,91	Sherry and Connie	3,4,5,6,10,12,13,23,24,31, 32,34,36,37,38,45
Kathy Lukin -Groom's aunt & Godmother	62	Pastor Lee Eclov	3,6,46,49
Darren O'Neil -reader	3,6,10,46	Greg Ursta -brother of the bride	56,57,58,59,90
Denise Silon -singer	87,104,102,101,76,46,3	Beverly Chulpka -seamstress	68

Communication Plan - *Wedding Example*

Who Needs To Know	What They Need To Know	Who Needs To Know	What They Need To Know
Alisha and Torrie Lukin -greeters	96,97,46	Ron Ursta -father of the bride	3,6,10,20,24,26,45,49, 56,57,70,75
Stacey Ursta -sister of the bride and singer	3,4,5,6,10,20,24,45,46,56,57, 58,64,70,73,81,84,85,87,88	Groomsmen -Dan, John, Mark, Tim, Dave, Greg, Ryan	3,4,5,6,7,10,20,24,30,45,46, 49,56,57,58,59,64,70,73,75
John Cunning -best man	3,4,5,6,10,20,24,45,46,56,57, 58,64,70,73,81,84,85,87,88	Docker's -rehearsal Adinner restaurant	1,3,9,16,22,23,24,37,52,30, 51,53,82
Jerry McNellis -father of the groom	1,3,4,6,44,45,46,51,56, 57,67,85	Pat Girard -photographer	6,7,10,20,45,48,49,50
Chris Hall -church contact	6,41,42,43,44,45,89,94	Cindy Ursta -sister-in-law of the bride	3,6,10,17,18,20,24,26,40, 45,46,58
Constantina -hairdresser	77,78,79,80,81,83	Mr. B's -cake	9,10,11,12,13,14,15
Sue Kline -pianist	6,41,42,43,45,46	Out of town guests	3,6,10,20,24,26,34,36
Marianne -church coordinator	4,6,9,23,37,41,46	BJ the florist	4,5,6,10,63,65,66
Erik Scheimer -DJ	5,19,20,23,24,30,41,81,85	Bridesmaids -Cari, Stacey, Lisa, Shannon, Cassie	3,4,5,6,7,8,10,20,24,84,45, 46,58,70,71,72,73,74,75
Bonnie -B&B Banquet Hall	2,5,9,15,16,19,20,23,25, 26,28,30,37	Video Memories	6,8,10,20,41,45,46,47,48,49

Communication Plan - *Wedding Example*

How Will We Tell Them	Who Will Tell Them	Deadline
A short personal letter with detailed bullet points	Pat will write out a letter and send out this entire plan to each vendor	July 3rd -1 month prior to wedding day

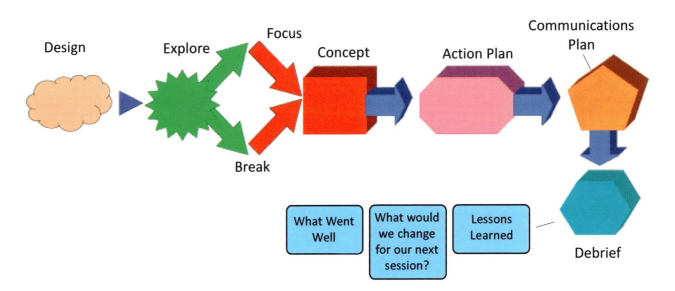

When debriefing a session these questions may help

- How were the facilities and atmosphere?

- How well did the design serve us?

- How did we perform our various roles?

- How well did we adhere to the Pure Form Thinking guidelines?

- How well did we spin raw thoughts into rich ideas?

- How well did we achieve the Purpose of the Session?

- How well did we fulfill the client's expectations?

- How well did we work within the time constraints?

- How well did we manage group dynamics/process issues?

- How well did we make our transitions between the parts of the Master Model?

- How well did we bring closure to the session?

Quick Reference Examples
PAGES 36, 46

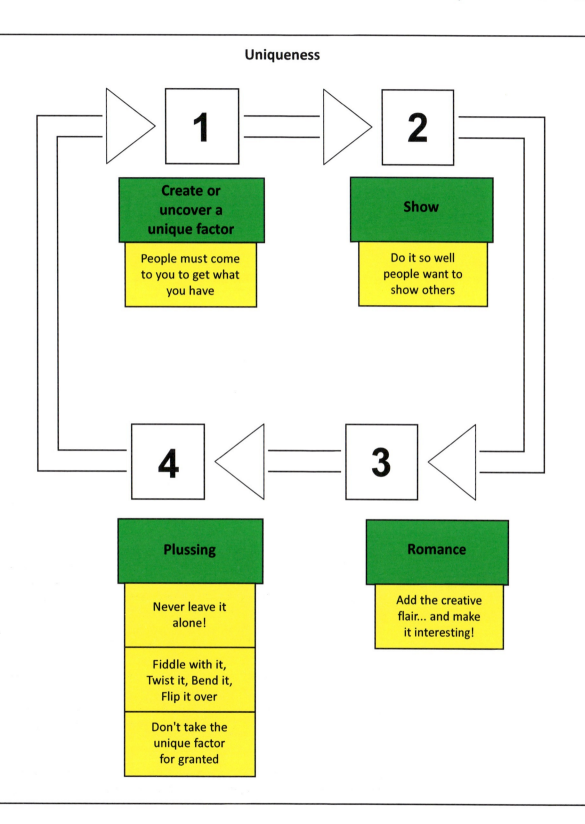

Austin Pacelli Shamrocks Fundraising Drive
311 4th Street NW
Austin, MN 55912
Pacelli Drive
Saturday, September 14, 2002

Written By Jerry McNellis

Background
Austin Pacelli, a parochial school in Austin, Minnesota, was facing tough times. It was being faced with the reality of having to close it's doors and put hundreds of students into the public school system. The disruption to the community by double shifting the public high school would have been massive.

A fund raising drive had to happen and it had to be successful. The fear of having a repeat of the previous year's efforts was overwhelming. A professional fundraiser had previously raised $60,000 and spent $40,000 doing it over a three month period. The small community of Austin, Minnesota was desperate as Pacelli High School was about to close it's doors.

Jerry McNellis
Jerry was recruited to design and lead the training for a fund drive and one last-ditch effort to save the school. When Jerry asked how the drive was organized, they asked if he would do that too.

After enlisting Jerry's close friend, Father Jim Buryskaa, they put together a plan that 12 days later raised $640,00 in 3 hours and with a $900 budget.

That was in spring of 1974. Today, Pacelli is still going strong.

The Birth of Compression Planning
How that fundraiser was tackled gave birth to a business that specializes in a high-speed way of working to tackle big challenges, messes and opportunities. Jerry started his business in 1978 and since then have been leading and teaching Compression Planning® to students and clients who are located six of the seven continents.

What follows are Jerry's recollections of the birth of his business.

Memoirs of an Entrepreneur and Visionary
"I didn't start out to build a business. I simply wanted to learn how to do things like the Pacelli drive. Where do you get training like that? No where – not then, not today."

As a young businessman it was apparent Jerry was going to spend a great deal of his time working on projects in meetings. And most of the meetings he went to were a waste of time. They took too much time and produced too little per hour of effort and resources spent. That realization led Jerry on a lifelong quest to learn how to do what eventually evolved into Compression Planning.

The Family tree of Compression Planning
Compression Planning is derived from three main sources. They are as follows:

1. Jerry's parents' influence in doing things in a unique way. Jerry remembers fondly as his father tells him "Don't do what others do. Do something different…and do it exceptionally well."

2. The Walt Disney Creative Planning and storyboard system Jerry learned from Mike Vance shortly after he left Disney. Mike was Disney's Director of Idea and People Development.

3. A system for planning and conducting meetings of boards of directors. Jerry and his aunt, Sister Terence McNellis (who was a school administrator) co-developed and trained thousands of people in a simple approach to making board meetings productive.

The first time Jerry used all three elements of Compression Planning together was the fund drive for Pacelli.

Non-Purpose Fundraising for Pacelli
They couldn't spend money. Anything else? As long as it was legal, the coordinators said they would back whatever J&J came up with…and they did.

A group like none other
Jerry and Jim then went on to recruit the team that would be tasked with the impossible – spend no money and raise buckets of it. They put together a group no one would have ever put around a table for raising money for a Catholic school. Jerry remembers that he and Jim were the only Catholics on the project team.

They recruited talent - mostly from the media. Kent was a Mormon. Dave was a journalist. Judy was on the evening news. Mike didn't know what the inside of a church looked like. They simply went for the best people they could think of who were able to do the basic approach that was laid out for them.

Top 10 Elements of their approach
1. Make it the buzz of the community by exploiting the public media
2. Use Pacelli high school as the headquarters – make it real
3. Organize and execute the plan so fast the opposition doesn't have time to gather forces
4. Take the message to potential donors ahead of time so they are fully prepared to contribute
5. Do multiple year commitments versus single years over and over
6. Make it so much fun and so exciting people want to participate
7. Involve as many people as possible – get buy-in from diverse groups
8. Make the messages simple and get them under control early in the process
9. Do everything in a unique way (remember Jerry's Dad's admonition)
10. Pray. Jerry and Jim knew it would take Divine intervention to make this a true, lasting success.

The following are the details of each of J&J's top 10 Elements

1. Make it the buzz of the community by exploiting the public media

Father Jim Buryska worked for the archdiocese and was intimately familiar with the church structure. He was an expert and this proved to be invaluable at times. Jim had also taught for several years at Pacelli which gave him a unique viewpoint.

Jerry had been running the local Chamber of Commerce for the past 5 years and had spent almost every Friday afternoon visiting the local newspapers, radio stations and TV stations. It helped that he had developed many contacts and friendships ahead of time with the public media.

Jerry asked them to volunteer and they pulled off some amazing things. Some of the media highlights were:
- Everyone wrote material to be shared with each other. They pulled their talent and shared openly.
- Everyone was involved in the creation of the media plan. The ones who were being asked to deliver the Pacelli message were in charge of developing it.
- Everyone functioned as a self-directed work team, not as traditional competitors. There was a common cause and they were committed.
- The publisher of the main newspaper, the manager of the radio station and the head of the TV station were briefed daily by either Jim or Jerry. They kept them informed.

2. Use Pacelli high school as the headquarters – make it real

Jerry and Jim knew they needed a large space to conduct their meetings, deliver the necessary training, and store all of the equipment. Most importantly, they needed space to kick off the campaign. Jerry states "I always go for a dedicated space for a campaign headquarters on fund drives. We have everything we need at our fingertips."

By using the school as their campaign headquarters, they had access to 100% of Pacelli's staff, students, equipment and the gym

They used the gym for the kickoff.

There was a lot of parking available for the many people that would be attending

Part of the plan Jim and Jerry developed included decorating the outside of the school with bed sheet banners the Pacelli students made.

The location of the Pacelli high school was on a high traffic street in town. Access to the school was easy.

3. Organize and execute the plan so fast the opposition doesn't have time to gather forces

Believe it or not, there was opposition to the fund drive. There was opposition to J&J's approach. There was plenty of bad blood among the three churches who sponsored the school. Jerry and Jim knew they had to so fast that the opposition couldn't rally any support to stop them. The opposition didn't have an alternative approach and came to support Jerry and Jim's plan.

The key coordinators originally they wanted another 3-month campaign. J&J's plan was to do it fast. People don't want to work on something forever especially if it's a fundraiser. Jerry and Jim's approach was simple - get in, plan it, do it, celebrate it and move on.

4. Take the message to potential donors ahead of time so they are fully prepared to contribute

The idea here was to help people make a decision *before* the actual fund drive. If this could be pulled off, then the campaign workers who called on them in their homes wouldn't have to be exceptionally well trained in the nuances of the issues around the school. The plan called for one adult and one or more students to visit each big donor.

The plan was not for those teams to be responsible for the "sale." This was especially important given the underground rumors going around.

The teams were told to just go out and get the checks or the pledge.

5. Do multiple year commitments versus single years

A key part of the fund raising campaign was to ask for *yearly* contributions. Why ask for single year pledges? Jerry and Jim decided to go for as much as possible and it worked. A key part of pulling this off meant that community leaders needed to back this drive.

This approach can be summed up as "maximize the return, minimize the effort." J&J developed a plan to leverage everyone's effort - one call versus three or four. It worked. Jerry wonders why his college doesn't just bill him annually for an alumni contribution versus calling me each. Send the bill. If it isn't paid, then follow-up.

Save the labor. Most people don't like doing fund raising unless they are pros.

6. Make it so much fun and so exciting people want to participate

People love door prizes…especially if they are worth something. The method J&J used to solicit door prizes saved a ton of effort in this fundraising drive. No one had to go begging. Jerry asked the manager of the local Sears store, Mike, to give them the money to buy a TV from a competitor. Mike's son was a student at Pacelli. Mike said he could and would donate a Sears TV; however, Jerry told him that would be expected and wouldn't accomplish the objective.

The plan was to have an anonymous contribution they could use to buy a much nicer TV from a competitor of Sear's who would never contribute a door prize to the cause. Mike choked. Then he wrote out the check after Jerry explained what they were going to do.

Jerry and Jim then held a press conference and said the first door prize for the workers and contributors was this magnificent large screen Magnavox TV. Jerry says he looked the reporters in the eyes and said the donor wished to remain anonymous.

Then guess what happened? The press ran with the anonymous story and the door prizes started gushing in. Jerry and Jim had to actually turn away donations for door prizes!

A Jewish car dealer donated a car and another businessperson contributed a new motorcycle. There were tons of high dollar door prizes. There was no collection effort. Leverage, lots of it.

Ideas like these permeated everything they did.

To get food for the workers they asked the little kids to be cookie monsters and make a dozen cookies each. They made hundreds of dozens.

The local McDonald's owner set up soft drinks as well as free coffee Jerry and Jim just trusted the food would come. It did.

To get food for the workers Jerry went on a joint radio broadcast the day of the drive. They were broadcasting continuously all afternoon. At 1:00 p.m. Jerry said if anyone wanted to help, sandwiches would be appreciated. If they would drive by the school with the sandwiches and honk their horn, a student would run out and get them. Later on in the day Jerry had to go on the air and ask people to stop bringing sandwiches, as there were too many to eat.

Any idea someone was excited about doing was done. Someone suggested giving away door prizes to people who say no. They did. It was a riot. Many who originally said no ended up as major contributors. Others didn't. There were so many door prizes that Jerry and Jim couldn't give them all away.

It was intentionally made fun for everyone who came anywhere near the campaign. It kept the time flying by, sometimes up to 16 hours a day, and kept the buzz flowing.

7. Involve as many people as possible – get buy-in from diverse groups

All ideas were seriously considered and if an idea was not used, the person who dreamt it up was told why it wasn't a fit. However, even if an idea was used, many times a part of it was woven together with another idea.

One of the ways they got students involved was having them preach in churches the Sunday of the campaign. That really worked. People were excited and enthused to hear students preach. The tough part was getting a couple of priests to cooperate. They eventually agreed to do it and were excited about the buzz that was created in their congregation.

Students also accompanied adults when calling on people for their pledges. The idea was that having the actual students there might soften anyone who would be nasty towards the volunteers.

Jerry and Jim simply asked the media for their help because they were the ones who had the skills.

Little kids were Cookie Monsters and made a dozen cookies each. People of all faiths and non-faiths contributed food for the hundreds of workers. People of all backgrounds contributed door prizes. People who contributed money and those who said no received door prizes Every student in the school was involved. Endless free labor.

9. Do everything in a unique way (remember Jerry's Dad's admonition)

The original pledge card (before J&J's team got involved) was a small one. Someone suggested that "little pledges are made on little cards; big pledges are made on big cards." So the little ones were thrown out and giant ones were made (12" X 24"). Jerry even got the local printer to donate the large pledge cards.

There was also a group of women representing the Philomatheon Society who donated $1,000 to kick off the campaign. Someone suggested having the president of the women's group escorted to the front of the auditorium by a gorilla. A local attorney agreed to rent and wear a gorilla suit to escort the tiny woman up on stage to make the kickoff contribution. They walked into the gym with her holding his arm. He was about 6'4". When they got close to the stage he spontaneously swept her up in his arms and she made the presentation that way. The gym was overflowing with students, workers, and musicians who were immediately laughing and full of energy.

There was also a chicken suit. After the kickoff, students took turns wearing the gorilla and chicken suits. One minute the gorilla would be tall. The next minute it would be short. Close to 50 kids worked in the costumes that day.

Wild and wacky ideas were being generated all the time. Someone asked "How can we do the prayer in a unique way?" Someone else suggested having a non-prayer. What would a non-prayer sound like? The answer was having the emcee call for a 3-minute silent prayer. Three minutes of silence! It was awesome and very appropriate. When the emcee said "amen", it was AMEN!

The Phone Company put 20 phones with special equipment into the school with only two days lead-time. The only out-of-pocket expense for the entire campaign was because the Phone Company couldn't swallow all the expense. They charged $900 for about "$50,000" worth of work.

10. Pray

Jerry and Jim knew the task would be an overwhelming one. They also knew that keeping a parochial school open would require some "divine intervention." Jerry says that to this day he doesn't fully understand the success of the Pacelli fundraising drive. He says much of it was due to the contributions of the hundreds of volunteers as well as the generosity of all of the donors. He and Jim also know that it wasn't just man who made this the success it was.

Miscellaneous thoughts – no rhyme or reason
I could go on because it was so filled with special elements, but won't. This experience was so rich in learning. My major insights came as a result of so many people saving Pacelli:

Every planning session we had we reviewed the Background and all other storyboards for everyone. We were moving so fast we wanted everyone on the same page at all times.

"The first person you recruit is the most important."
Father Jim was a natural and we complimented each other so well. We agreed early to always support and never question the others outside the planning time. It meant we didn't have to consult each other. If someone asked Jim something I automatically agreed to support it and vice versa.

Set the bar high when recruiting. Who wants to simply be on a committee?

We had to adopt a neutral/"serve them" mindset or we'd have been buried in the politics.

Know who your clients are and get focussed on the most basic issues. Know the boundaries such as not being allowed to spend money.

Discover early what isn't in your assignment.

Get your client(s) behind you early on

Go for the best people – not by position, pedigree or background. Just get the best for a tough job. They will rise to the challenge.

Get your basics in place before going into detail. Make sure your WHAT is lined up before you do the HOW details.

Amazing how people support each other on high quality teams

Keep the leadership fully informed. Don't let them get blindsided.

Uniqueness - *Fundraising Example*

Go beyond the traditional message carriers as they are frequently more effective.

Get adequate space for the job. It is amazing how often this isn't thought of until it is too late.

Everything has competition and you need a plan to deal with it.

Look for COMPRESSION. Always more effective.

We thought recalcitrant donors would be more polite on the adults contacting them for money with students present. The kids knowledge and enthusiasm sure helped.

Explain the rationale behind your requests. Share the method behind your madness.

Be specific with your requests.

We were so confident it would work. We didn't have a backup plan.

This campaign wouldn't have made it without a non-judgmental attitude during the idea sessions.

Normally people aren't saying do my idea. Rather they are saying consider my idea. Close the loop with them. Whether you do their idea or not. Explain why not. Have a reason.

We asked first through third-graders for help. Involved lots of parents and grandparents.

Pay attention to the embedded messages you send.

Ask "how can we do this in a unique way?" Consider 180 degrees from the expected approach and the results are usually quite effective.

Amazing what you can get when you ask. I had a 6-page list of specifics when I met with the head of the phone company to do something I knew was impossible under normal circumstances. They delivered 100% on time.

P.S. My favorite story in the campaign is one I alone experienced.

The school was pandemonium that Sunday afternoon. Someone asked me to go to the lobby of the school. There was a man, woman, and two small kids. Both parents were holding armfuls of bags from Country Kitchen restaurant. They were traveling from Ohio to visit their parents in South Dakota and heard my request for food for the campaign.

So they got off the interstate and bought all this food to help. I took the food and handed it to students to take to the kitchen. Someone tapped me on the shoulder for something and when I turned back to talk to the family they were gone. I ran into the lavatories looking for them. I went all over trying to find them to say thanks and get them on the radio and before the media.

When I went outside they were gone. Gone. I couldn't find them. So I went to the kitchen to make sure I wasn't hallucinating (it had been 12 days with hardly any sleep) and there were 6-8 large bags of food with Country Kitchen labels.

P.P.S My other favorite story was at the end of the kickoff session. The environment was electric. Hundreds of people were in the gym/campaign space. Music...cheerleaders...a gorilla holding a presenter. Etc. etc. etc.

Then we had the drawing for the large screen TV. The drawing was just for people in the gym at that moment. We did that to get everyone to the kickoff on time.

When the winner's name was read a universal scream went out by the students. The winner was a young man from a huge family (16 kids or so) and everyone almost instantly knew he was from the best family to win. Later on I found out they didn't have a working TV.

Once the screaming died down the MC said "Go do the job."   People almost tore the doors from the doorjambs.

P.P.P.S.   I wrote this from a secular point of view. I always believed the Almighty was leading the drive.   Father Jim Buryska and I had the privilege of being there to learn by doing.

Project Teams - *Definition of Roles*

Roles within a Project Team

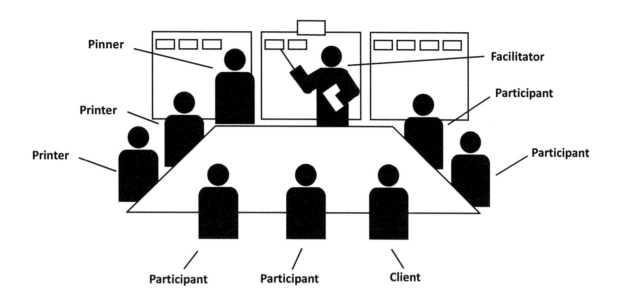

Pinner / participant
1. Dumps the push pins out on the table
2. Pins subber cards in the center of the card

3. Avoids overlapping and gapping cards
4. Stands to the side when waiting to pin so the participants can see the boards
5. Contributes ideas during a session
6. Does not act as a second facilitator

Printer / participant
1. Uses a verb as first word on a card
2. Captures a single, complete thought per card
3. Prints, DOES NOT WRITE
4. Listens and waits for the spin
5. Contributes ideas during the session
6. Asks for help when uncertain about what to print

Participants
1. Avoid playing off the client
2. Focus their entire energy and thinking upon issue at hand
3. Listen and build on others' ideas
4. Direct energy to content not process

Client / participant
1. Owns the project
2. Sits where there is low eye contact with participants
3. Focuses their entire energy and thinking upon the issue at hand
4. Contributes, but does not dominate

Facilitator
1. Conducts the session
2. Gives direction to PINNER and PRINTERS
3. Gives permission to take risks
4. Protects people and their ideas
5. Brings out the best thinking of the group
6. Manages the group's energy and the process
7. Coaches convergence and closure

© McNellis & Associates • Compression Planning Institute • 724-847-2120 • www.compressionplanning.com

Recruiting Project Teams

Principle 1 Recruit to Purpose
- Since each session Purpose changes, involve people who can best deliver the desired outcome
- Recruit a "friend of the court"

Principle 2 Seek diversity
- Male/Female
- Age
- Departments/Roles
  i.e.-Marketing/Finance
- Knowledge/Perspective
  -Ex-Perts
  -Co-Perts
  -In-Perts
- Stakeholders
- Free Spirit
- Years in the organization
- Different levels within the organization
- Ethnic

Principle 3 Consider outside resources
- Vendors
- Customers
- Consultants currently under contract
  -Ad Agency
  -Bankers
  -Freight Company
- Friends

Principle 4 Challenge the assumption of the natural work team
- Many natural teams lack the knowledge and perspectives which allow for effective sessions

Project Teams - Model #1

Finding and Setting up a Temporary Warehouse

Background
- Sketch of current warehouse
- Photos of the mess
- Charts of expected needs

Overall Purpose
- To find 50,000 square feet of dry, safe space
- To be operational in the new space in three weeks

Purpose of this Session
- To identify all the key pieces of the plan

Non-Purpose of this Session
- To discuss the need for a new warehouse
- To discuss the three week deadline

Permission Meter

HEADERS

- What are our requirements
- Sources to contact
- Equipment needed for new space
- People issues we must consider
- Parts of our company impacted by the move
- What are the timing issues
- Who needs to be involved to pull this off
- Misc.

Client: WAREHOUSE MANAGER

Date: WITHIN THE NEXT TWO WEEKS

Time Frame of This Session: 2-3 HOURS

Number of People In Session: 5

© McNellis & Associates • Compression Planning Institute • 724-847-2120 • www.compressionplanning.com

Project Teams - *Model #1*

Suggested Project Team

Permission Meter

Name	Title
T.G.Z.	Warehouse Manager
F.P.D.	Night Shift Supervisor
C.R.T.	Scheduling Coordinator
D.U.D.	Trucking Company Representative
S.W.F.	Fork Truck Operator
R.L.S.	Commercial Realtor

© McNellis & Associates • Compression Planning Institute • 724-847-2120 • www.compressionplanning.com

Project Teams - *Model #2*

Helping our Realtor to sell our home

Permission Meter

Background
- Photos of home
- Inside
- Outside
- Aerial
- Map of our area

Overall Purpose
- To realize $225,000 from the sale
- To sell the home within 60 days
- To have at least 30 qualified potential buyers go thru the home within the next 45 days

Purpose of this Session
- To find 5 things our realtor can do immediately
- To find 4 things we can do

Non-Purpose of this Session
- To talk about changing realtors
- To discuss lowering the asking price of the home

- Hints for fixing up our house that people will notice
- Dramatic ways to present the house
- Ways to light a fire under the Realtors
- Ways to use unconventional advertising ideas
- Misc.

Client: FRED & ETHEL
Date: NEXT SATURDAY
Time Frame of This Session: 2 HOURS
Number of People In Session: 4-5

© McNellis & Associates • Compression Planning Institute • 724-847-2120 • www.compressionplanning.com

Project Teams - Model #2

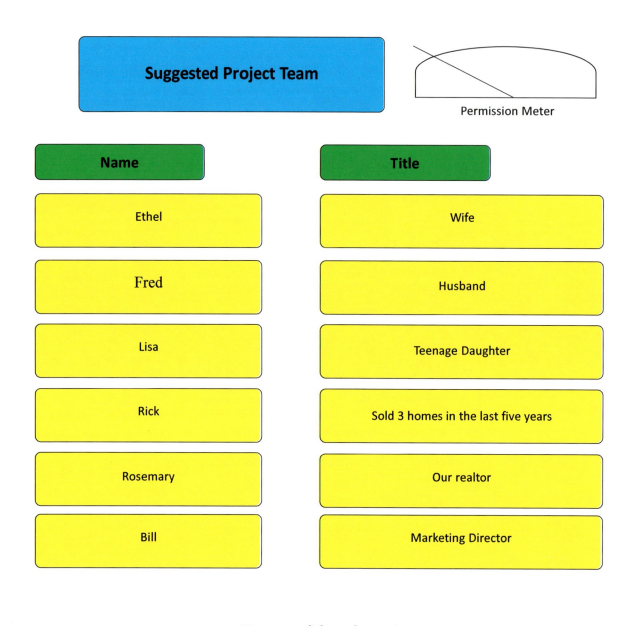

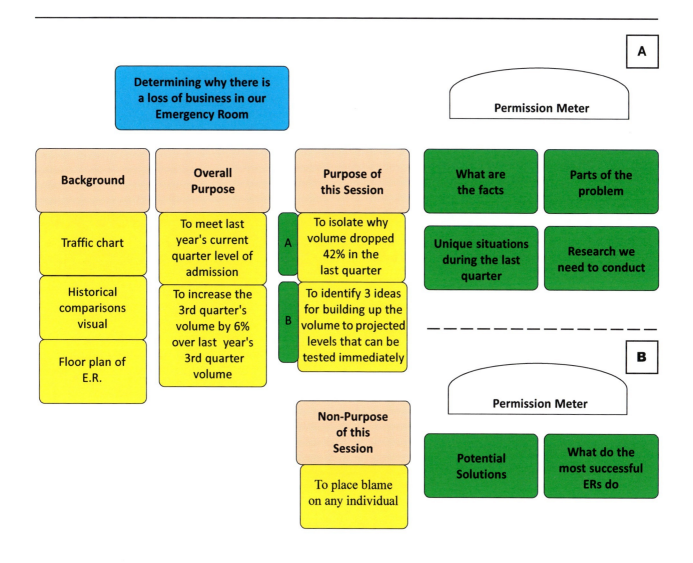

Client: JUDY OSBORNE – E.R. DIRECTOR

Date: NEXT WEDNESDAY

Time Frame of This Session: 8:30 - 11:30 A.M.

Number of People In Session: 7

Project Teams - *Model #3*

Suggested Project Team

Permission Meter

Name	Title
Tom Bozic	ER Director
Julie Olson	ER Nurse
Millie Shank	Department Director
Horace Book	Ambulance Crew Chief
Ollie South	Admitting Person
Osgood Schatter	Senior X-ray technician
Bradford Titch	Recent patient

Ways to validate the topic

- Good/Bad our ER at different times
- Hang around bus depot
- Talk to President of company whose sales fell 40%

© McNellis & Associates • Compression Planning Institute • 724-847-2120 • www.compressionplanning.com

Facilitating a Session

- Complete design...Pages 16-31
- Use McNellis Design Alert......................................Pages 134-137
- Recruit project team...Pages 118-119
- Gather tools/supplies..........................www.storyboardtools.com
- Set up room..Page 131
- Conduct session...Pages 68-87
- Call The Compression Planning Institute for help or to brag!!

Hints...Do:
- Begin within 7 days
- Facilitate your first projects on a subject and with people who will help you be effective
- Use the design form and use it step by step
- Refer back to your seminar notebook
- Limit your first sessions to 8-10 people
- Build your skills
- Keep in a learning mode
- Keep a low visibility
- Know it takes 24-48 months to get storyboarding into an organization

What to avoid...Don't:
- Be overly enthusiastic about storyboarding
- Get hung up on it
- Use it when you already know the answer
- Do more than a $2 \frac{1}{2}$ hour session the first time
- Pick emotionally loaded projects for your first topics
- Make a big deal out of the process
- Take on the most complex issue in your organization
- Put it in the newsletter

© McNellis & Associates • Compression Planning Institute • 724-847-2120 • www.compressionplanning.com

Launching A Session

Before the Launch
1. Set up the planning space
2. Finalize set-up of the storyboards
3. Set out the tools - Cards, pins, dots, etc
4. Check room temperature and make adjustments

At the Launch
1. Have introduction (if required)
2. Briefly explain:
    a. Your role as facilitator
    b. The storyboard process
3. Recruit printers and pinners
4. Have client walk to storyboard and go through design
5. Ask for clarifying questions. Have client / participants give answers
6. Direct printers to put additional clarifying answers on cards to be pinned under background
7. Explain Pure Form Thinking and review guidelines
8. Have pinner put Exploratory guidelines on storyboard
9. Explain and negotiate the use of the "Reminder Balls/Artifacts"
10. Start facilitating the first Header

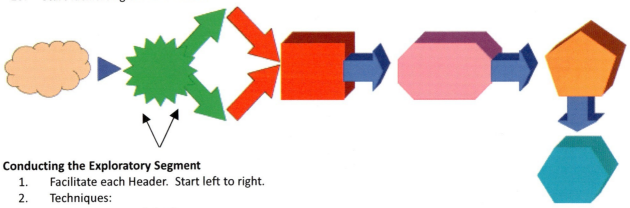

Conducting the Exploratory Segment
1. Facilitate each Header. Start left to right.
2. Techniques:
    - Spinning
    - Sub-divide
    - Switch perspectives
    - Switch Headers
    - Ask content or process questions

The "YAMA" as adapted by McNellis & Associates

History

- Beginning in 1916, the Conference Board began leading retreats with major business executives
- Retreats originated at YAMA Farms in the Catskills of New York
- The facilitator drew each individual's name out of a famous "YAMA" hat
- Participants shared relevant insights and comments directed to the theme of the conference

When to use a "YAMA"

- When you want all members of the group to address an issue
- When a session ends and you want participants to offer final comments
- When you want to deal with how the group is functioning
- When you as a facilitator are stuck

Possible questions to ask group

- "Right now I am not sure where we are headed, share with us a thought which might unlock us"
- "The group is struggling, what are your thoughts (or feelings) about what is going on?"
- "We have not been able to focus into a firm concept. What do you see as our next step?"
- "As we conclude, what suggestion/word of advice/conclusion do you wish to make or offer to the client?"

Steps for a successful YAMA

- **Step 1**: Print each group member's name on a yellow card (or have each person do it)
- **Step 2**: Shuffle the cards
- **Step 3**: Determine a question you want to ask. Do you want to evoke thoughts or feelings?
- **Step 4**: Ask participants to respond when their name is called
- **Step 5**: Ask a question and then pause for a half of a minute or so, so the participants have time to form a response
- **Step 6**: Specify how much time each participant has for their response
- **Step 7**: One at a time call on each person for their comments
- **Step 8**: Take the client's card out of the sequence and call on them last
- **Step 9**: Encourage people to listen to each other without responding

© McNellis & Associates • Compression Planning Institute • 724-847-2120 • www.compressionplanning.com

Bringing closure to a 2-3 day Compression session

Here are some thoughts on how I would close a session:

"Well, we've all worked extremely hard the last couple of days and we've come down to our plans, developed the key ideas, resolved some critical issues, have an action plan and a communications plan.

We've evaluated how we've worked together as a team. Now, this is your last chance to just speak ot hte other people around the circle. These comments aren't aimed at the facilitators or the McNellis Company.

Speak to your colleagues. Take about a minute a piece. What thoughts do you have to close our time together?"

Suffle the name cards and read them off one at a time. I look ahead a bit and find the client cards and put them last. I also include the McNellis staff for their closing comments, so if you have people helping you, let them be part of it.

You'll learn surprising things
The YAMA will tell you as much about the session in may instances as the debriefing. There have been times I thought the session really wasn't as great as I had hoped, and during the YAMA, I learned phenomenal things happened that I wasn't even aware of as the facilitator.

A YAMA can be used during the session, both content or process or learning-wise. I have the cards printed out ahead of time and I carry them with me. People in the group can call a YAMA, or as a facilitator, I can call one.

Floating an issue free
For instance, if there are 12 people and I see two or three are heavily engaged in an issue, I'll call a YAMA and make sure everyone gets their viewpoint expressed. I'll also call a YAMA if the group is at an impasse and can't get around some issue. Frequently the YAMA will float the issue free.

The advantage of the YAMA over asking each person to comment is that they begin rehearsing instead of listening. With the random order of a YAMA, they have to be alert. You'll just find a much more spontaneous response.

Asking the right question
At the advanced session, participants were asked to come up with questions they have used, or could see themselves using in a YAMA. Some examples are:
- "How are you feeling about this effort at this time?"
- "What is the common ground that links our different positions?"
- "Imagine yourself walking along a road and coming to a field that is fenced off. What has happened today that feels like that fence, and what would it take to open that gate?
- "Tell us how you think you will feel about this session three days from now."
- "What needs to happen for us to move forward from here?"
- "Looking back at today, what does it make you want to do when you wake up tomorrow?"

You'll probably find that the dynamics of your session and group will steer you toward your questions. Don't be afraid to ask!

Compression Planning Center Overview

Track Lighting   **Storyboards**   **Blackboard and Easels**

Comfortable Chairs   **Refreshment Center**   **Resource Center**

© McNellis & Associates • Compression Planning Institute • 724-847-2120 • www.compressionplanning.com

Storyboard Suspension System

We've developed a simple and inexpensive system for hanging the storyboards. A bolt assembly, pictured below, is placed in the top corners of the storyboard. The board is then suspended from a "J-track" - available from any carpet store. The track should be hung 80" from the floor and attached to the wall every 20".

Don't wait for the perfect facility to begin planning though. Put storyboards on easels or prop them on chairs, but get going! The more results you have with the process, the more commitment there will be for setting up a permanent planning center.

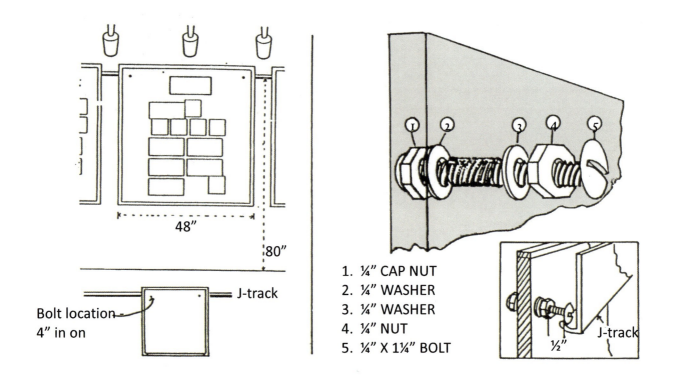

1. ¼" CAP NUT
2. ¼" WASHER
3. ¼" WASHER
4. ¼" NUT
5. ¼" X 1¼" BOLT

DESCRIPTION

Macklinburg Duncan Tapdown metal
<u>without</u>
teeth in SILVER (or available in GOLD)

What is a Design Alert?

- A free follow-up, consultative service to anyone who has completed the Compression Planning Institute.
- Special help is provided in all phases of a Compression Planning Session. Help in the Design of a session is most frequently requested
- A McNellis Compression Planning Specialist will contact you within 24 hours after your Design Alert is received

When you need help

- Call 724-847-2120 and tell us that you have a Design Alert
- If you want to talk with a particular Compression Planning Specialist, feel free to request their help
- Before calling, complete a design form so that you are prepared to share the information
- We request that you E-mail or FAX your design to one of our Compression Planning Specialists, along with a statement of what assistance you need
- After studying your design, the Specialist will call and talk through the project with you

Points to remember

- Allow as much lead time before your session as possible
- Tell us if you need help immediately. Sometimes travel schedules make it difficult for a Compression Planning Specialist to reach you in less than 24 hours, but we will do our best to handle your request
- Make yourself accessible for our response. Leave your work and home telephone numbers and the best time to call at each location. Notify work colleagues we will be calling and alert them to help us reach you

Design Alert - Definition and Instructions

Information needed when you send your Design Alert

[Topic Card]

[Background] [Overall Purpose] [Purpose of this Session] [Header] [Header]

[Header] [Header]

[Non-Purpose of this Session]

- Topic
- Background (list it out)
- Overall Purpose
- Purpose of this Session
- Non-Purpose of this Session
- 3-5 Headers
- Permission Meter

- Date of Session
- Time frame of Session
- Number of participants

- Client

- Your:
  - Name
  - Office phone number
  - Home phone number
  - Email
  - FAX number
  - Cell Phone
  - Best time to reach you

© McNellis & Associates • Compression Planning Institute • 724-847-2120 • www.compressionplanning.com

Reflections on the countless Design Alerts I've personally done over the years
- by Jerry McNellis

Don't ever feel you are imposing. We love doing them and I believe it makes our teaching and assistance stronger..

The first things I check are...
1. How specific is the Overall Purpose. Is it measurable, quantifiable or verifiable? If it isn't, we discuss ways of tightening it.

2. Then I go to the Purpose(s) of the Session and ask the same questions: are they measurable, verifiable and quantifiable.

3. Then I check your number of participants and length of the session. I want to make sure the amount of work expected from the session, the number of people and the number of Headers are reasonable.

4. Normally people want feedback on their Headers. I frequently suggest fewer Headers - 3-5 or less for many issues that are being addressed in less than 2 hour sessions. Longer sessions are an entirely different issue.

KISS IT - *I try to help people simplify their designs.*

HEADERS
The language in the Headers is also something I review. Is it too complex, full of jargon or in/out of alignment with the Purpose(s) of the Session?

Are the Headers stated so they will actually deliver the Purpose of the Session? Sometimes people have interesting Headers but they won't deliver the expected outcomes. There needs to be a logical fit to all of these elements.

PERMISSION METER
I check the permission meter to see the connection between the specific Purpose of the Session and the headers - is there alignment?

MISC.
After taking notes, we call you and discuss your design.

At times we do design alerts by e-mail. Pat McNellis does a lot of them this way and then will follow-up with a phone call.

All of us have different styles but follow the same basic procedure.

My style is to use a Design Alert as a coaching experience for you and a learning one for me. I nit pick designs in a way facilitators seem to really appreciate.

My intention is to give extremely specific feedback of a positive nature and to point out areas for improvement.

Just pointing out flaws isn't our approach. I think it is important you know specifically what we think you are doing right.

Briefing Board - *The System*

Briefing Board

Do | **Doing** | **Done**

Task $____ (multiple)

Input

Task $____

Hang-Ups

Task $____

TASK

- Date initiated (top left)
- Due date (top right)
- Date Completed
- To whom assigned
- Budget or actual costs $____

© McNellis & Associates • Compression Planning Institute • 724-847-2120 • www.compressionplanning.com

Generating a Quick Compression Planning Report

Patrick McNellis oversees the function of getting the reports to our clients after our facilitating a CP session. He either does the work or subcontracts it and makes sure it meets the standards needed before getting the final report to a client.

The following is Pat's advice on how to generate a quick report. His record, to date, is getting 60 storyboards into one report and having it in the client's email inbox before 8:00 a.m. the next day.

Patrick McNellis' Insights on CP Reports...

The companies and organizations we work with want a real fast report versus something slick and glossy that takes time to develop.

I've spoken with Compression Planning Alumni who are using other programs to generate reports, but I personally prefer a simple word processor – in our case, Microsoft Word.

Preparing your space to generate the report

Now, I know this sounds simple, but clear off your desk before you start! You'll be spreading piles of cards out and you want to make sure you keep them in sequence.

If you have a storyboard near your desk, then use it to pin the taped columns of cards up. I usually just take a piece of tape and tape each column on the wall in front of me. I can fit five columns on the wall in front of me which saves time.

There are two things that will make your life a lot easier in tracking the input of your report. First, I always lay out the envelopes (which I marked with a number before taking the taped cards off the storyboards) in the sequence I need to input them. I then have large envelope or a small box that I put the smaller envelopes in after I am done inputting the cards.

Before I put the envelope in the box/large envelope, I put a check mark on the smaller envelope which let's me know I am done with that particular envelope. It sounds simple, but when you are inputting a large report, it's the small things like this that make it a lot easier.

The 3 Golden Nuggets of a CP Session Report

When putting together your report, there are three parts of the session that really drive the report. They are your Concept, your Action Plan and your Communications Plan. These parts are the "meat" of why you "meet" or rather, met.

When putting together a report, this is typically how it goes together.

1. Start out with a Title Page. Where do you get your title? Your topic card! It's also a good idea to put the date, the location and who facilitated the session on this first page.

Generating a CP Report

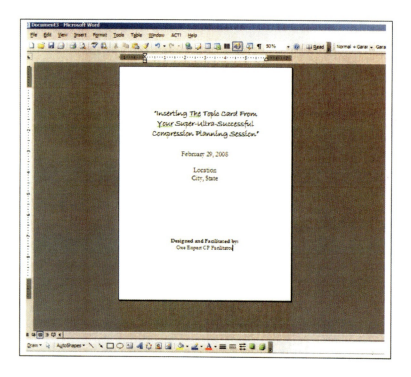

2. The next page is typically the Table of Contents. This is usually developed as the LAST step in putting together the report.

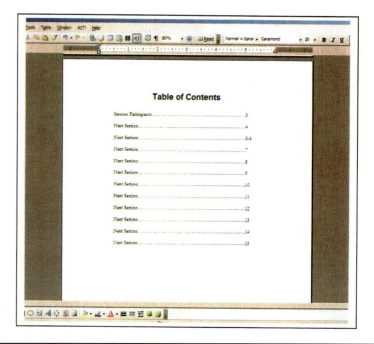

3. Page 3 is always a Participant List – who was there and who facilitated and helped.

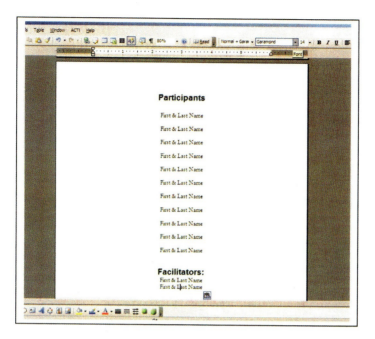

4. Page 4 can then be the original Design/Agenda you followed with the group.

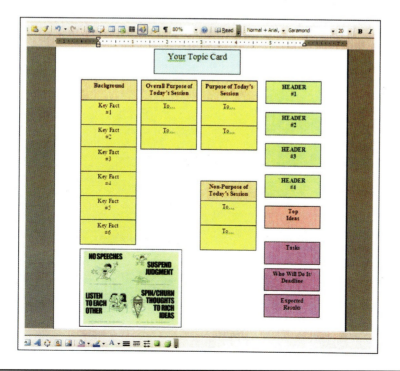

You can use text boxes and color them in to get the "visual effect of your storyboard." If you do your design like this before your actual session, which often helps a client "see" what it's going to look like, you can just do a quick copy and paste into the report.

I don't do the entire report like this for several reasons. You may need to rearrange data several times and it gets too "messy" and difficult if you use the text boxes. Second, it takes too much time and the payoff isn't worth it.
It does, however, look nice if you include just the design in your report. It gives it the "storyboarding flavor" that straight text does not.

5. I recommend the next section be your Concept – your session deliverables. You can put some text to it if it helps tell the story. "The group met to identify the key issues surrounding the purchase of "xyx company." Or "The following are what the group agreed were the top issues."

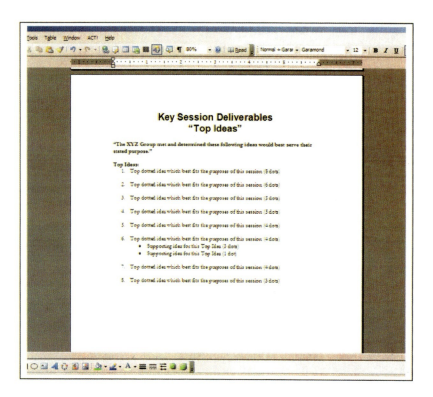

I always put the number of dots in ( ) at the end of a dotted idea.
For example: Propose discretionary funds ($100 petty cash fund per month) for each line that doesn't need "upper management approval" - (6 dots)

There will be times when you use two (or more) different colored dots. If this is the case, then just put the colors after the number. Just make sure you include a legend of what the different colors mean.

Using the above example again:
Propose discretionary funds ($100 petty cash fund per month) for each line that doesn't need "upper management approval" - (6 blue dots, 5 red dots)
Legend: Blue Dots = Supervisor, Red Dots = Management

6. The next page in your report should be your Action Plan. I find it easiest to use tables when doing this.

Make four columns with the first being Tasks, followed by Who Will Do It/Deadline in the middle one, followed by Expected Results in the third. I include a fourth column for Updates/Status. It gives you the flexibility to track deadlines being met or delayed and the ability to document why.

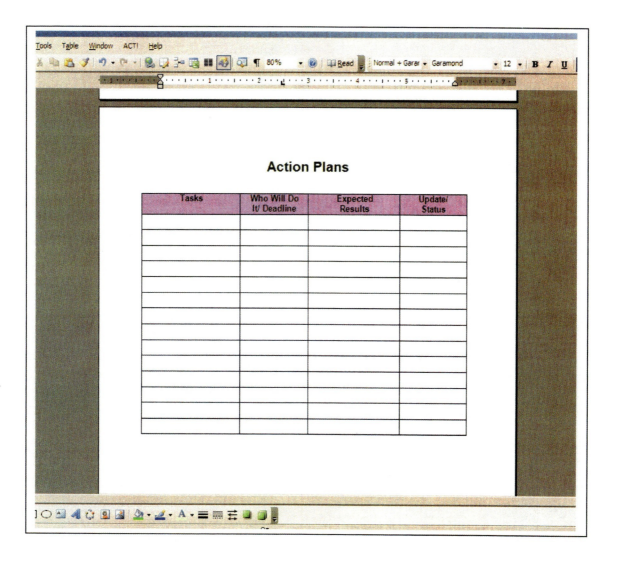

7. The next page should be your Communications Plan. It's easiest do to this by first numbering your messages and then putting the rest in a table format.

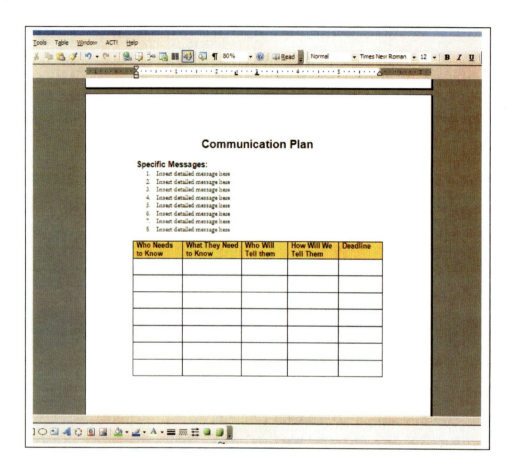

You'll want to give more detail to your messages when you generate the report. You may have had a card that said "Time, date and place for the upcoming training" that went up during your session. Now is the time to make sure you have the details – the actual time, the actual date and the location.

You frequently give a shorter message during the session that needs to be spelled out a bit more as a part of the report.

Up to now, this is the meat of your report – the major deliverables. If you are pressed for time to get a report done and out the door, get at least these three parts done.

The Rest of Your CP Session
There are several reasons you'll want to document everything from your CP session though. They are as follows:

1. There will be ideas that can't be done right now but could be done 180+ days from now that didn't make it to your "concept."
2. By documenting everything, you are forming a knowledge management system.
3. As a reference point when you review or revisit your topic at some point in the future.

I usually have a title for this section that goes something like this – Miscellaneous ideas developed during the session that didn't make it to the 'Key Deliverables.'

I recommend bolding your header question and using simple bullet points that are indented. Don't forget to put the number of (dots) at the end of the idea.

For Example:
This is your Header Question
- This is your idea with the number of dots included (12)

I personally don't worry about arranging the cards from highest dotted item to lowest until after I am done inputting the cards. Word has a very cool function that allows you to quickly rearrange your ideas. If you highlight the line (or even just put the cursor on the line it will end up highlighting itself) and then hit shift + alt + the arrow keys, you can either move an idea up or down.

If you used your Retrieval Envelope, make sure you don't forget to enter the cards from there. I usually have a heading that says "Retrieval Envelope" and then I bullet point the cards that are in there.

At this point, when you have everything inputted from your session, go back and fill in the page numbers and details for your Table of Contents.

That, my friends, is a CP report.

For more information, contact:
Patrick (Pat) McNellis
(724) 847-2120
pat@compressionplanning.com

Compression Planning 'Table-ology'

There are a lot of things that go into making a Compression Planning session work and they aren't always on the surface and obvious.

This BrainTrain is about one of those "not-so-obvious-components" – specifically, the characteristics of ideal Compression Planning tables and how best to set them up.

When it comes to Compression Planning, you want your tables to do three things for you:

1. Be comfortable to sit at and not impede participation - correct size with legs that aren't "knee hazards"
2. Position the client out of the power seat. Put them in the corner. You want the flow of your session to be directed to the storyboards, not filtered through your client.
3. Be configured in a manner to be able to see the storyboards while still facilitating discussion - not classroom style.

Advanced Site Preparation

One of the many things on our logistical checklist is a room set-up. We want to to arrive at our location and have the room arranged how we need it to best serve our client. Any good hotel or conference center will ask you for a room set-up.

Once we know the amount of space we'll be working with, the next question we ask is "What size tables do you have and where are the legs positioned on the tables?"

The ideal table is 8 feet long by 30 inches wide with the legs inset enough to allow someone to sit at the 30" end of the table comfortably.

Here are two options for groups ranging in size from 8 - 12 participants. Remember that the pinner will not always need a seat, but one should still be provided.

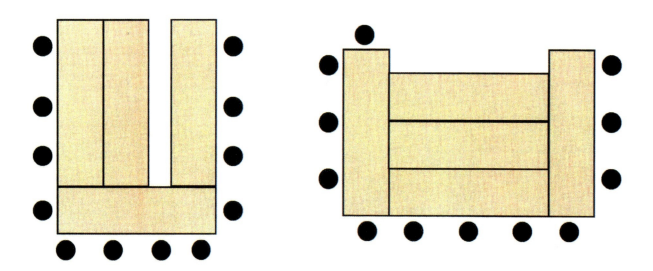

Characteristics of an ideal Compression Planning Table

An ideal table has the following characteristics:

1. Lightweight - can be easily moved if needed.
2. 30" wide. You want enough space for people to be comfortable with their "stuff" as well as having a glass of water or coffee.
3. Legs that are positioned so that your participants won't bang their knees.
4. Either 6 feet long or 8 feet long with 8 feet being the preference.

The ideal set up for a group ranging in size from 8-12 is a "modified horseshoe."

A Compression Planning Table Critique

Table A:
This "rounded" table is difficult to put into a U-shaped configuration due to it not being rectangular. It would be fine for a breakout table.

The space between the legs would make it easy for a person to sit on the ends and not worry about their knees.

Rating: ★★

Table B:
Bad, bad, bad. Not possible to connect to another table and make it work.

A lot of tables now have something going down the back - some for computer cables, some for "looks." Either way, you can't sit someone on that side so this won't work.

Rating: ★

Table C:
Too small. I'm showing this table due to it's width. It's an 18" wide table. You'd need to put two of these together to get a comfortable table for drinks and materials.

The legs are also at the end which, even with two together, would not work.

Rating: ★

Table D:
Nice and wide and the legs are inset. This is a unique table that would be interesting in a conference room where you'd have several that could make a nice U-Shaped.

My only concern is that it might be too heavy and awkward to move if needed. ★★★★

Table E:
This is the kind of table you frequently find in a hotel or conference center. It will need a table cloth as the wood usually gets banged up easily.

I like this table because you can sit someone on the ends and it's nice and wide. Too bad it's ugly.

Rating: ★★★

Table F:
I've used these many times and I love these tables. They look ok, hold up well, and are light and easy to move.

Ok, you may not want these for your board room, but for a dedicated meeting room, you can't go wrong. Perfect size and width and placement of legs.

Rating: ★★★★★

© McNellis & Associates • Compression Planning Institute • 724-847-2120 • www.compressionplanning.com

Dedicated Meeting Space

"The ideal table configuration creates an intimate setting where people can see and read the storyboards. It also helps facilitate discussion."

This typical boardroom table is the archenemy of Compression Planning facilitators. They are too big, often too bulky and take up too much space.

Due to the size of many of these tables, and the sizes of the chairs you frequently find in board rooms, there just isn't enough space to do a Compression Planning Session.

This table, on one hand, is beautiful. It's positioned right next to a row of windows, beautiful light wood and it just looks cool.

However, can you imagine actual discussion going on here? It's another perfect example of a "rubber-stamp-boardroom."

But is sure does look nice!

Two of our great clients have transformed their boardrooms with modular sets of tables like this one. It looks good for the board plus is easily adaptable for other uses...specifically Compression Planning Sessions.

There are six tables in this configuration that can easily be moved and adapted for your group.

© McNellis & Associates • Compression Planning Institute • 724-847-2120 • www.compressionplanning.com

Things to stay away from

1. 18" wide, skinny conference tables.
2. There are lots of classroom tables that are great for lectures, but not for a CP session.
3. Set in place boardroom tables - these are difficult to facilitate a CP session because they do not break down, you can't move them, and they tend to be HUGE and take up an entire room.

Some other things to keep in mind

1. When setting up your tables, make sure there is good lighting in the front which will illuminate your storyboards. Be prepared to relocate your tables if the lighting is poor. We've arrived at conference centers and the room set-up was perfect...except for the lighting.
2. Modular tables can be used in a board room which is also a dedicated planning space. They look nice and they work well. Modular tables are those that can be configured in several different types of configurations - kind of like a puzzle.
3. Horse shoe settings work for groups ranging in size from 8-24. If you go larger than 12, set out a few single tables that fan across the back of the room so you can subdivide the group and they have a place to go work. See the following example:

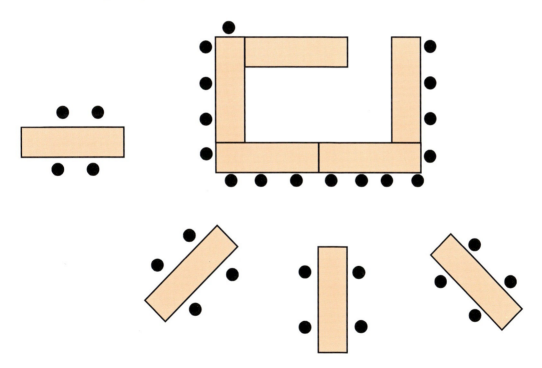

The following pages have 3 room set-ups for jobs we have been contracted to facilitate. They ranged in size from 20 - 75 participants.

Group Size:
50 people

ROOM SET-UP

Please use 8'x30" tables for all grouped table configurations - grouped and single.

Contact Information:
McNellis & Associates
Patrick McNellis
724-847-2120

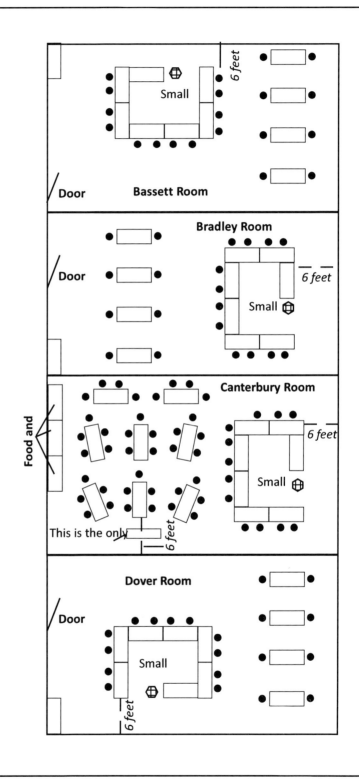

Table-ology

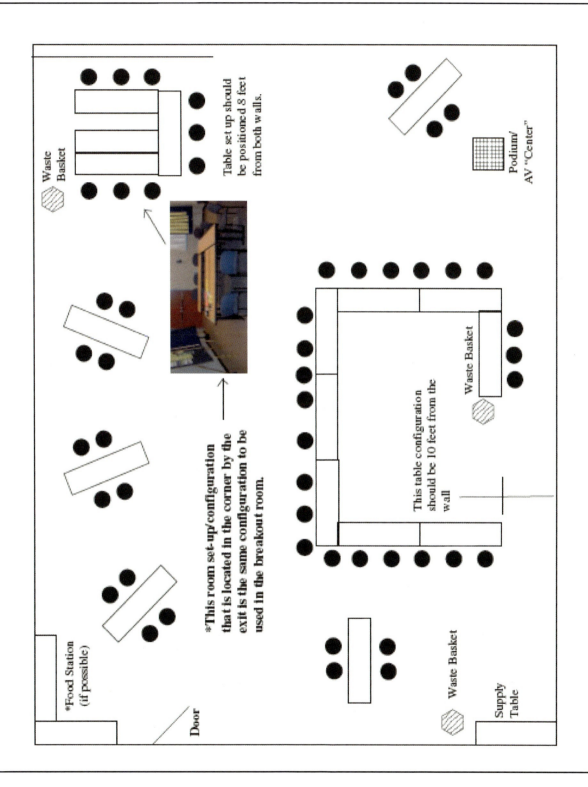

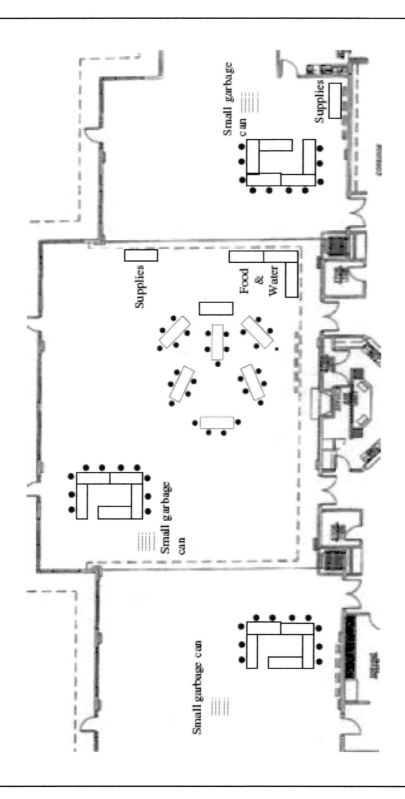

In a recent workshop, we had a participant who told us something she shared with her husband on the first day of the training.

Her words were…*"You know, I couldn't believe you started out the workshop teaching us about push pins. I went home and told my husband 'you're never going to believe this…they are teaching us how to correctly use a push pin.'*

We both agreed you were a bit "particular" about the little details (actually used a different word that I'm sure you can imagine!).

After going through the entire workshop, it now makes sense why you are constantly reinforcing those "101 level" things. I had to go back and share with my husband why it actually made sense about being so 'particular' with the push pins!"

Tables are another one of those "101 level" things to look at for a Compression Planning Session. A good table configuration makes it easy to work with a group. It's my hope to share with you all of those little 101 things that will help you best serve your group effectively.

About the Author
Patrick McNellis

In 1992 Patrick McNellis challenged the materials that made up the manual that was being used for the Compression Planning Institute. It was, he thought, rather thin.

That started him down a pathway of collecting all of the Compression Planning knowledge that was out there and putting it in a format that was user-friendly and easy to understand for future participants.

Pat has always been interested in how skills learned in a "workshop" transfer back and manifest themselves in the workplace. He has taken this interest and has spent hundreds of hours developing this book to serve as a "reference manual" for graduates of the Compression Planning Institute. Knowing that after the workshop there would be questions about dealing with certain situations, Pat developed this comprehensive "database of Compression Planning knowledge" to help smooth the way through new planning ventures.

Pat McNellis is a "helper" at heart. He's a gifted facilitator and coach and thoroughly enjoys helping friends and colleagues think through "tricky" issues – whether they are professional in nature or personal. He is often sought after to help friends develop high-impact resumes and cover letters and his track record for "getting the interview" has been remarkable. He credits Compression Planning and digging for the uniqueness as the foundation for this success.

When Pat does not have his Compression Planning hat on, he's enjoying raising his toddler twins – Logan and Lauryn – along side his best friend and wife, Stephanie.

Contact Information:
pat@compressionplanning.com
724-847-2120

To learn more about the McNellis Company services and products...

Visit the following Web sites:

www.compressionplanning.com
www.mycpcommunity.com
www.exeutivedecisionmakingsystems.com (you'll find Jerry's blog for senior leaders here)

For more information about the McNellis Compression Planning Advantage, including the Compression Planning Institute, contact Institute Concierge Stephanie McNellis at 800-569-6015 or at Stephanie@compressionplanning.com.

If you are interested in learning more about having McNellis professional facilitators design and lead a Compression Planning session for your key people on a "pivotal issue," "strategic questions," or a "huge opportunity," please contact Pat@compressionplanning.com.

If you would like to inquire about having the McNellis team conduct Compression Planning training for your business or organization at your desired location, please contact Dianne@compressionplanning.com.

If you'd like to talk with Jerry McNellis, send him an e-mail at jerry@compressionplanning.com or call 724-746-1220.

We highly recommend **Storyboard Tools** as your source for storyboard supplies. We buy and rent from them and they are our backstage provider, so you can rest assured that they are first class and dependable.

For more information on products, contact:
Storyboard Tools - www.storyboardtools.com
Kim McDemus - kim@storyboardtools.com
1445 Washington Road, Suite 400
Washington, PA 15301
Phone: 724-229-0954 or Fax: 724-229-3052

McNellis & Associates
715 15th Avenue
Beaver Falls, PA 15010
724-847-2120
800-569-6015

© BRAINTRAIN PRESS
All rights reserved.   No part of this publication may be
reproduced, stored in a retrieval system, or transmitted
in any form without the permission of McNellis & Associates.

Made in the USA
Charleston, SC
26 November 2012